Potions

by Kerri Connor

ALPHA

A member of Penguin Group (USA) Inc.

For Tammy and Kristy,
Thanks, you two. Your support is unbelievable!

ALPHA BOOKS

Published by the Penguin Group

Penguin Group (USA) Inc., 375 Hudson Street, New York, New York 10014, U.S.A.

Penguin Group (Canada), 10 Alcorn Avenue, Toronto, Ontario, Canada M4V 3B2 (a division of Pearson Penguin Canada Inc.)

Penguin Books Ltd, 80 Strand, London WC2R 0RL, England

Penguin Ireland, 25 St Stephen's Green, Dublin 2, Ireland (a division of Penguin Books Ltd)

Penguin Group (Australia), 250 Camberwell Road, Camberwell, Victoria 3124, Australia (a division of Pearson Australia Group Pty Ltd)

Penguin Books India Pvt Ltd, 11 Community Centre, Panchsheel Park, New Delhi—110 017, India

Penguin Group (NZ), cnr Airborne and Rosedale Roads, Albany, Auckland 1310, New Zealand (a division of Pearson New Zealand Ltd)

Penguin Books (South Africa) (Pty) Ltd, 24 Sturdee Avenue, Rosebank, Johannesburg 2196, South Africa

Penguin Books Ltd, Registered Offices: 80 Strand, London WC2R 0RL, England

Contents

Introduction

Potions have gotten a bad rap in the past, but the age-old art is making a tremendous comeback. That's because more and more people are recognizing the magical and medicinal properties of herbs and other natural ingredients. Combine such mixtures with a specific intent, such as to increase energy, achieve success, heal, or even find love, and you have a potent brew.

You have probably already used potions hundreds or thousands of times without even realizing it. For instance, ever had one of those neon-colored energy drinks after a race or during an intensive workout? Most of these contain a blend of guarana and ginseng, herbs that are known to increase energy. These specialty drinks are essentially potions, it's just that they are manufactured in mass quantities and marketed to a specific audience.

Or open your bathroom cabinet, pick out a couple of bottles, and look at their list of ingredients. Most shampoos, conditioners, lotions, and liquid soaps contain herbal extracts, and so are all potions designed to benefit the user in some way.

Although we don't usually call energy drinks, shampoos, teas, and other natural mixtures *potions*, that's what they are: a potion is simply a combination of natural ingredients that contain medicinal or magical properties. (Don't worry, I'll talk about what it means for something to have magical properties in Chapter 1.)

This book will teach you everything you need to know to get started on using and making your own potions. I cover everything from the history of potion making, to their modern-day uses, and along the way I introduce you to dozens of common and not-so-common ingredients and their magical properties. Although I provide you with the tools you need to create your own recipes, I also give you several recipes that are known to be effective for achieving specific aims.

A Bit of Magic

If you are new to magic, you may be wondering just what exactly it is. Magic is a form of energy. It resides inside of you, inside of me, inside of animals, and inside of plants. As a matter of fact, every single living organism has magical energy inside of them. Some people learn how to harness this energy and use it, while others deny its existence and never get to experience their own glorious magical abilities. Since you are reading this book, you obviously want to know more about harnessing your magical energy to improve your life!

Magic can take a number of different forms. Let's take a look at a few of the more common magical practices.

Spells

A spell is similar to a prayer. It is a request sent out to the universe, including any deities—Gods, Goddesses, High Powers—you work with. When casting a spell, you build up the magical energy inside of you by focusing on your intention, and then release the energy into the universe. The use of herbs, oils, incense, and potions are all ways to increase this energy and to help you focus on your intention.

Spells may be elaborate and contain the use of tools and magical ingredients along with spoken words, or they may be as simple as wishing upon a star.

Divination

Divination is the practice of finding answers to questions through magical meanings. There are many forms of divination, including tarot card readings, runes, pendulums, scrying, and using a crystal ball. The type of divination you use dictates how the practice is performed. For instance, you interpret tarot cards' meanings by studying the pictures on the cards and/or relying on standard interpretations, whereas divining using scrying and crystal balls involves focusing intently on the question and watching for an answer to appear.

Rituals

Rituals are usually performed for one of two reasons: either to celebrate an event or experience (usually in a form of giving thanks), or to ask your deities for a specific blessing. I include a brief blessing ritual in Chapter 2.

Extras

As you read through the following chapters, you'll encounter the following sidebars, little extras that are intended to help you perfect your potion practices.

Toil and Trouble

These boxes contain important warnings and precautions to take while preparing and using your potions. Following these precautions will keep you and anyone else who uses your potions out of harm's way.

Concoction Clues

Here you'll find hints, tips, and shortcuts to help you prepare and use your potions as effectively as possible.

Enchanting Explanations

Here you'll find background information or other interesting tidbits about the topic at hand.

Magical Definitions

Like any specialized area, the art of potion making and magic has its own lingo. I define any terms that might be new to you in these boxes. These and other terms are also defined in the glossary.

You're Ready to Get Started!

With this book, you are equipped to make and use potions to your advantage, while enhancing your magical abilities and spiritual connections.

Trademarks

All terms mentioned in this book that are known to be or are suspected of being trademarks or service marks have been appropriately capitalized. Alpha Books and Penguin Group (USA) Inc. cannot attest to the accuracy of this information. Use of a term in this book should not be regarded as affecting the validity of any trademark or service mark.

From the Cauldron to the Kitchen

In This Chapter

- Demystifying potions
- Taking a brief look at the history of potion making
- Understanding why potions have a bad rap in some circles
- Using potions today

To really understand what potions are and how they are used today, we must turn back the pages of history to the era before the rise of the Catholic church, when Paganism was the mainstream form of religious practice. We must explore how and why potions went out of fashion, and then take a look at their revival in recent years.

This brief history will provide a rich background for the rest of the book, where you will learn the correct ways to prepare and use potions for your own purposes.

Potions of the Past

Potions have been subject to widely shifting cultural attitudes. During Pagan times, potions were the primary means of healing and were well respected. With the spread of Christianity, however, church leaders discouraged the use of the magical elixirs, calling them the work of the devil.

Magical Definitions

A **potion** is a combination or mixture of ingredients that contain medicinal or magical properties. Although a potion is mainly made up of liquids, some solid material might be present.

The First Potions

The origin of potion making is lost in the mists of time. Basic concoctions involving herbs and other natural ingredients, such as bark and nuts, probably date back to the beginning of human existence, with those earliest efforts involving a lot of trial and error to determine which combinations of ingredients were effective. When the potion maker struck upon a successful elixir, he or she would pass the recipe on to subsequent generations, first orally and later, with the development of written language, in written form.

Then, as today, potions were used for just about anything—from maladies to magical spells. Potions were used for everything from soothing a raspy cough to easing pain to bringing good luck, fortune, or love to the user.

Enchanting Explanations

The art of potion making has never really gone out of style, it has just taken on different names. For example, the perfume industry makes potions designed to attract attention to the wearer!

Pagan Practices

Many Pagan traditions believe that the knowledge of potion making was given to humans by fairies or the Gods and Goddesses as a reward for good deeds. Although there is no way to confirm this story, we do know the use of potions was an important part of Pagan practices in the pre-Christian world.

Medicine or Magic?

A cup of chamomile tea will soothe an upset stomach. Lavender oil in bath water will help relieve stress and enable you to relax. Are these concoctions magic or medicine … or both? Such distinctions didn't exist in Pagan times, when potions were a combination of magic and medicine.

Enchanting Explanations

The Pagan blending of magic and medicine into a single concept is evident in the term witchdoctor, a person who uses magic to cure illnesses.

Not all potions were meant to be beneficial to the user, however. Indeed, some were meant to be harmful, and it is this darker side of potion making that in part contributed to the practice's negative reputation. Even some potions that were meant to be helpful might have had unintended negative effects on the user.

In ancient societies, the task of potion making usually fell to women, often older women, who served as healers. A healer could spend her entire life learning, practicing, and teaching others how to use the magic from the earth to help others. These older women were seen as "wise women" who passed their craft down to their daughters or others so the practice could be carried on.

Healers collected and grew the necessary herbs and created potions and other items to bestow good health and good fortune on their patients.

Healers prescribed potions to cure illness, to attract prosperity, to help crops grow, to make a woman conceive, to protect children, or to banish an unwanted person from one's life.

Paganism Comes Under Fire

Paganism began to decline with the advent of Christianity. In particular, the Catholic church had a profound impact on Pagan practices. Originally known as Gentiles, by the end of the fourth century, the term *Paganus* was used instead to describe the country dwellers who continued to use magical practices.

Magical Definitions

Paganus is a Latin word meaning "country dweller"; it now refers to people who practice a polytheistic religion, which many of the country dwellers did.

In the fourth century, Constantine was appointed Emperor of Spain and issued the Edict of Toleration, which gave Christianity equal status with Paganism. He eventually prohibited the practices of divination and magic (this included the making and use of potions) under penalty of death.

Constantine's son and successor, Constantius, furthered his father's work by ordering all Pagan temples closed and declaring that anyone found guilty of offering sacrifices would be put to death.

In 364, Valentinian I became emperor, and he issued four edicts prohibiting the practice of magic, making even the study of magic punishable by death.

Enchanting Explanations

It is important to remember that history is written by the "winners." The vast majority of accounts we have about Paganism in ancient times come from the writings of those who worked to defeat Paganism while promoting the Church. We should expect some of these accounts to show a bias favoring the side of the Church, since it was the Church that for the most part "won."

Over the years, more laws were issued against Pagan practices. Temples were destroyed instead of closed, and any Pagan practice was declared a penal offense.

The Rise of the Church

In the sixth century, Martin of Tours argued that Paganism was the result of ignorance, and he spent his life trying to "educate" the people. He condemned all Pagan practices along with any other type of magical workings, including, of course, the craft of making potions.

By the eleventh century, Catholicism was the dominant religion in Western Europe. However, Paganism wouldn't just go away. Instead, it went underground, into hiding.

Toil and Trouble _____

Just as many Pagans do not want to be judged by the actions of their ancestors (such as animal or human sacrifices), it is not fair to judge Christians based on the long-ago actions of their forebears.

The Burning Times

By the time of the Spanish Inquisition, often called The Burning Times, in the thirteenth century, anyone even suspected of using herbal folklore for cures (or curses!) was considered to be a witch (a type of Pagan) and therefore a devil worshipper. Strangely, though, the vast majority of people, mainly women, who were executed during that time were not Pagans at all, nor were they guilty of the acts of which they were accused. Explanations for why so many women were falsely accused of Paganism include the growing distinction between magic and medicine. Doctors (who were men) saw their practice as a science and therefore more safe and "real" than the so-called superstitious practices of herbal remedies, which were usually practiced by women.

The divide between magic and medicine that started to emerge around the time of the Spanish Inquisition became more distinct as the centuries went by, in large part due to the rise of academically trained scientists and physicians. Eventually, the divide became so wide that magical potions and medicine were considered to be part of separate ideologies.

Enchanting Explanations

Many innocent people were killed during The Burning Times. Estimates range from the conservative 100,000 to the liberal 9 million. Although most of the accused were women, men and children were also accused and executed.

By no means is this a complete history. It is simply intended to give you an idea of the battle to eradicate Paganism and magical practices. Many attempts over the centuries were made to convert Pagans to Catholicism. Those who didn't convert were punished in other ways, including seizure of property, prison, and even death.

The Pagan Revival

Over the past 50 years, Paganism has been on the rise in the Western world.

A quick search of the Internet will turn up hundreds of Pagan groups, stores, books, and magazines. And although many Pagans still hide their beliefs and are "in the closet," many more are open about their beliefs. The study of herbs, oils, and aromatherapy (all of which are Pagan topics) are all on the rise, too.

Enchanting Explanations

Due to the nature of Paganism, it's very difficult to count the number of practitioners; and with many in the closet, we might never know for sure just how many there are. Some estimates claim there are over 3 million Pagan practitioners worldwide. Paganism has been described as the fastest growing religion in the Western part of the world.

As Paganism grows, so does the need for people to reconnect with nature and natural healing processes. Making your own potions is a large part of this reconnection process. Throughout this book, you will learn how to make an assortment of potions to help you. You will begin to bridge the gap between magic and medicine and understand potions as our ancestors did.

Modern-Day Brews

Modern potions can be used for either magical or medicinal purposes. Some will easily fall into either category, as they have properties of each. Some brews are made for external use only (such as for poultices); others (such as teas) are safe for consumption.

Medicinal Potions

Medicinal potions are for physical ailments, such as headaches, indigestion, fatigue, nervousness, and arthritis. Chamomile tea, known to have a calming effect, can be a medical potion to relieve anxiety.

Toil and Trouble

It is important to note that in the United States, the Food and Drug Administration (FDA) has not evaluated the medical effectiveness of most natural herbs.

Magical Potions

Magical potions deal with nonphysical problems such as emotional, spiritual, and financial difficulties. Potions may also be used to aid in building relationships, though it should go without saying that a potion should never be given to someone without their knowledge of what the potion is made from and what its intent is. Some examples of magical potions include the lotion you rub onto your hands to draw money toward you, or the dab of perfume you use behind your ear to entice your mate.

You can, however, use potions to make you more appealing to others, help you lose weight, or increase self-esteem.

 **Toil and Trouble**

It is highly advisable to have an allergy test done before becoming too involved in potion making. You don't want to handle plants you are allergic to!

Potion Versatility

Many potions have both medicinal and magical properties. For example, a potion to help you lose weight can fall under both categories as it helps to create a physical change, yet at the same time fall into the magical category because as you lose weight you will feel better about yourself.

The Importance of Intent

The most important element in any potion—medical or magical—is your *intent*. Intent is not only what you want the potion to do for you; it is why you want the potion to have the given effect. Seemingly harmless potions can have disastrous results if the intent is hidden, not clear, or used to do harm through deceit.

Magic should only be used for good, positive results. To ensure that this is the case, you must sit down and clearly think about your wishes before going on to perform any magical work at all. Your energy will be going into your potion, so you need to make sure you know exactly what kind of energy you want going into it!

> ### Magical Definitions
>
> **Intent** is the main ingredient in your potions. You must know why you are making the potion and what it is you want it to do. Do not make any potions with the intent to harm.

This book focuses on potions for magical purposes. However, because there is an overlap in some kinds of potions, a few of the discussed potions will also have medicinal properties.

In the next chapter, we begin to learn the basics of preparing potions for use, including the tools you need and what precautions you need to know about ahead of time.

The Least You Need to Know

- A potion is a mixture in liquid form that can have medicinal and/or magical properties.
- Potions have a long history and have taken on many different forms over the years.
- The intent of the potion is its most important ingredient.
- Never give anyone a potion without his or her consent.
- If you do give a potion to someone else, you must disclose its ingredients and intent.

Chapter **2**

Potion Preparations

In This Chapter

- Distinguishing between internal and external potions
- Identifying and using the right tools
- Harnessing the power of the moon
- Taking necessary precautions
- Understanding the importance of intent

Just as it's very difficult to bake a pie without a rolling pin and a pie tin, it's difficult to make a potion without certain pieces of equipment—what I like to call my potion-making tools. Potion makers use an assortment of tools—some essential, others less so—to prepare their concoctions. In this chapter, I introduce you to the essential items in any potion maker's tool chest.

One of the most important elements for successfully preparing potions isn't a tool at all. Instead, it involves your mindset, or your intention. I delve into this issue, as well as several potion-making precautions, later in this chapter.

But first, let's take a look at the two most basic categories of potions: those that are safe for human consumption and those that are not.

An Assortment of Potions

As stated earlier, a potion is a mixture of items in a liquid form that contains magical and/or medicinal properties. Some potions are safe for human consumption. These are called *potable potions*.

 Toil and Trouble

Always make sure you know the nature of every ingredient in your potion, including whether it is safe for human consumption. If you harvest the herbs yourself, be sure you know exactly what the plants are. You don't want to accidentally ingest something that is harmful.

Some potions are not meant for consumption, but instead are used in baths, soaks, poultices, cleansers, or lotions. These are called *nonpotable potions*.

Drink Me! Potable Potions

Potable potions are any potions that may be taken internally. These include teas, infusions, tinctures, and other beverages or "palatable potions." A fruit smoothie, jam-packed with natural ingredients, is definitely a type of palatable potion!

It should go without saying—but I'll say it anyway, just to be on the safe side—that if you're planning to imbibe your magical brew, then you must make sure that all your ingredients are safe for human consumption. If you aren't sure if it is safe to ingest a certain plant, either find out or, better yet, use another one instead.

Knowing whether or not a plant is edible isn't quite enough, though. You also need to know whether or not you are allergic to it. Some allergies are mild and only cause a runny nose, but other allergies can cause anaphylactic shock, which can be deadly.

Nonpotable Potions

Nonpotable potions are meant to be used externally. These include bath teas, foot or body soaks, lotions, potions applied to a cloth to use as a poultice, perfumes, liquid air fresheners, household cleaners, and much more.

 Concoction Clues

You should always label all of your potions, indicating their purpose and listing all ingredients. You can go one step further by developing a system to tell you at a glance whether a potion is potable or not. For example, use a smiley face for edible mixtures and a frown face for nonedible potions.

As with potable potions, you must make sure your ingredients are safe to use. Don't use ingredients you aren't familiar with, and beware of allergens. Soaking in a lavender bath won't relax you if you are allergic to it!

Tools of the Trade

As you learned in Chapter 1, the tradition of making potions goes back to the beginning of human history. Certain tools have long been associated with potion making, and people who want to feel close to that tradition sometimes use those ancient devices. Others prefer to use more modern implements, including electric appliances, to save time and effort.

No matter whether you use traditional or modern tools, I highly recommended you use them only for making potions. Because potion making is a magical process, you don't want to dilute the magical properties of your tools by using them for mundane, everyday purposes. You can buy a chest to keep them all in and store them safely.

Knives and Bolines: Slicing and Dicing

You need a blade for cutting herbs.

Traditionally a *boline*, a knife with a curved blade, is used for harvesting and cutting herbs. The curved blade cuts herbs better than a standard straight-edge knife. Bolines come in a variety of styles, though traditionally they have a white handle.

Magical Definitions

A **boline** (bow-LEEN) is a knife with a curved blade used to harvest and cut herbs. Traditionally, the boline has a white handle.

If you buy your herbs instead of growing and harvesting them yourself, you probably do not need to invest the money in a boline, as you won't have much use for it.

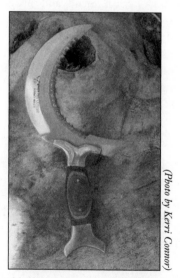

(Photo by Kerri Connor)

A boline used for harvesting herbs.

Even if you do grow and harvest your own herbs, you don't need a boline. Any type of knife that is capable of cutting your plants will do. The important thing is that whatever tool you choose for cutting, you use it exclusively for potion making. Obviously, some plants have thicker stems, so a stronger, larger knife might be necessary, but other plants with slim stems might even be clipped with scissors.

Mortar and Pestle: Grinding and Mixing

A mortar and pestle are actually two tools that are used together to crush, grind, and mix ingredients. A mortar is a very hard, thick bowl with a large mouth and a smooth bottom. A pestle is a thick rod with a slightly rounded end that is made out of the same material as the mortar. The pestle is used for crushing or grinding the ingredients against the inside of the mortar.

(Photo by Kerri Connor)

The mortar and pestle is used for grinding herbs into a powder.

Most mortars and pestles are made from marble or another hard rock. You can also find them made of wood, although these are not as widely available. If you are adventurous you can try making your own. Otherwise, you should be able to find sets at your local metaphysical store, or at any of the hundreds of online stores specializing in Pagan products.

Although many people find it extremely satisfying to use a mortar and pestle to grind ingredients, the process can be time consuming, and it also involves some elbow grease. A few modern-day equivalents to the mortar and pestle can make your work much easier and save a lot of time:

- A small grinder/chopper can be used to create fine powders.

- A coffee bean grinder set on espresso grind will give you a very fine powder. I love my grinder and use it for making incenses, too. It works well if you have anything really hard to grind such as cinnamon sticks or, of course, coffee beans!

Concoction Clues

To dry herbs quickly and avoid the chance of molding, you can use an electric dehydrator. Just follow the instructions for the dehydrator and in a day or two you will have perfectly dried herbs to grind or chop for use in your potions or other recipes.

- A food processor is also good for chopping up herbs, especially dried herbs, as well as fruits and vegetables. A food processor doesn't give you as fine a grind as a coffee bean grinder.

- A blender is ideal for making potions that need to be either pureed or well blended. Blenders work best with soft foods, such as bananas, tomatoes, and any food that has been softened by being cooked first.

- If you plan on making potions using a lot of juice, you should invest in a juicer. An electric juicer extracts the maximum amount of juice from fruits and vegetables, and the juice is much fresher than any juice you will find in a store, with no preservatives or other additives.

  Even if you use a juicer, you still need to use a blender when combining different juices to make sure they are mixed together very well.

 **Concoction Clues**

Remember that juice obtained through a juicer does not contain additives. It will need to be refrigerated and will not have a very long shelf life unless you freeze it.

As with all your tools, these appliances should only be used for your magical workings. Using magical tools for mundane purposes weakens their energy, and allows for easy contamination with negative thoughts and feelings. Although this might sound expensive, most of these items can be picked up at your local discount department store for about $10 each.

Cauldrons and Censers: Cooking and Burning

A cauldron is simply a large round pot, usually made out of cast iron. Many have three legs, so the pot can stand on its own, and a handle for hanging over a fire. Cauldrons are used for boiling water and heating potions.

(Photo by Kerri Connor)

Cauldrons are available in many different sizes.

Obviously for most people, it isn't very practical to hang a cauldron over an open fire or in a fireplace, but if you have access to either sources of heat, go for it! Not only is it fun, but it gives you a sense of being connected to our ancient ancestors.

You can find large cauldrons, along with hanging stands, on the Internet and at many camping supply stores. If you order one and have it shipped, be prepared for a hefty shipping fee, as the larger ones are quite heavy.

Instead of a cauldron, you can use any pot that is large enough to serve your purpose. If you just need hot water, you can also use a teakettle.

Whereas a cauldron is generally used during the process of making your potion, a *censer* is used with the final product to release its magic into the air.

 Magical Definitions

A **censer** is a nonflammable container used for burning incense or a charcoal tablet. A potion might be sprinkled onto the lit tablet to release the potion into the air through smoke.

A censer is a nonflammable dish, plate, or bowl made of metal or heat-resistant glass. Some censers have lids with holes for the smoke to flow through. You can also find censers with chains for hanging.

(Photo by Kerri Connor)

Censers come in a variety of shapes and sizes. Here, a metal gravy dish from a thrift store is shown as an inexpensive option.

When using a censer with your potions, you will need to use charcoal tablets. There are many different brands on the market that light very easily, and they can be found just about anywhere that sells powdered incense.

When using a censer, place a charcoal tablet on it, and light it with a long match. You might find it easier to hold the tablet with tongs as you light it and then place it in the censer when it begins to spark. In about 10 seconds the sparking will stop and the tablet will begin to glow, meaning that it is lit. If only half of the tab glows, use a pair of tongs to pick it up and then try lighting the unlit side.

Toil and Trouble _____

If your charcoal is getting old, it might take several tries before you get it completely lit. This is a sign you need to buy some new charcoal!

After the charcoal is completely lit, sprinkle whatever it is you want to burn on it. A censer is generally used for powdered incense or dried herbs, but you can also use a very small amount of a nonalcoholic potion, or a potion made with a mixture of essential oils.

Be prepared for steam or smoke and be sure to only use a small amount at a time so you do not burn yourself or extinguish the charcoal. I highly recommend using only small amounts of essential oils; do not mix them with any carrier oils, as you will not like the smell the carrier oils give off. (For more on oils—including the difference between essential and carrier oils—see "The Essence of Essential Oils," later in this chapter.) When dripping essential oils onto a charcoal tab, a little goes a long way! Although it won't sizzle for long, the scent will linger for quite a while.

Concoction Clues

If you have a censer with a chain, you can walk with the censer and very gently swing it back and forth. This is convenient if you are using a potion for a protection spell involving a large area such as your home or your property line. This will ensure the potion and magic is released all over instead of in just one area.

Bottles and Vials: Put a Cork in It!

Bottles, jars, and vials for storing your potions are available in all sorts of colors, designs, and shapes. When deciding what kind of container to use, first consider what is in your potion.

With some of the potions, you won't make the complete potion all at once. For example, when you prepare a tea, you first make the dry ingredients and then add that mixture to hot water as needed. When you add the dry ingredients to water, you have finalized your potion. Until then, you need to store the dry tea mixture in an airtight container. Wide-mouth jars with screw-on lids are perfect for tea. The wide mouth makes it easy for you to spoon out the amount you need to use.

(Photo by Kerri Connor)

Bottles and vials to store your potions in are available in all shapes and sizes.

When you complete your potion, you can pour it into a bottle with either a screw-on cap or cork. Brewed teas and other potable potions should be used within a few days of making. Your other potions can also be stored in this same manner.

Bottles, jars, and vials are easy to come by. The easiest and least expensive option is to reuse bottles that contained other products. I have found most of my bottles this way; some of them used to contain some sort of alcohol, such as brandy or liqueur, and so they already had cork stoppers, and many have interesting shapes and colors. Used jelly or jam jars work well for smaller amounts, and pickle or mayonnaise jars work for larger quantities.

If you want to buy brand new bottles and jars, check the Internet, kitchen supply stores, or craft stores. For years, I found beautiful colored bottles with cork stoppers on clearance after Christmas sales.

No matter what kind of bottle or jar you use, make sure you wash it well and sterilize it—you don't want your potion mixture that you store in an old pickle jar to smell like pickles! For used jars, I also paint the lids to hide what the original product was and to make it more decorative. You can add any other embellishments you like. After that, you will need to bless or consecrate the container with a ritual. After this is done, the container should only be used for your magical workings.

Blessing Your Tools

All of your tools and the chest in which you store them should be blessed, magically purified, and consecrated to their use in making your potions. After they are blessed, you should use them exclusively for your magical practices.

The ritual you use may be as elaborate or as simple as you like. A simple ritual could involve asking your patron deity or deities to bless the tools while running them through sage smoke.

Enchanting Explanations

In addition to purifying and blessing your tools, you should purify yourself. A pre-ritual cleansing bath is used to purify your mind, body, and soul. Use this time to forget about everything else. Turn off the phone, lock the door, play some soothing music. This is a time to relax and to begin focusing on your ritual ahead. All other thoughts should be set aside. To help achieve your aims, add to the water a magical ingredient, or component, that corresponds with your intentions. We go over the correspondences to some common components in Chapter 3.

Here is a brief and easy sample ritual for consecrating a magic tool. In this example, we use a mortar and pestle.

Light a sage smudge stick and set it into a fire proof dish or cauldron. Hold your mortar and pestle in the sage smoke and say, "Great Goddess and Great God (substitute the names of the deities you work with if you would like), I come to you to ask for your blessing upon this tool. This mortar and pestle, which will be used to grind herbs for my magical workings, is an extension of myself. I consecrate this mortar and pestle to the workings of my magic."

Moon Water

Full moon water is a preferred ingredient in many potions because it is charged with the natural powers of the moon. You can make full moon water by placing tap or spring water outside (in a sealed, clear container) with the full moon shining down upon it. You can reserve this specially-charged water for washing your tools, herbs, or other ingredients, or you can use it in the potions themselves. For example, I use full moon water in my tea to give it extra power. Full moon water is best used in potions designed to aid in perfecting ideas, working on positive aspects, increasing psychic and physical energy, and enhancing creativity.

New moon water is ideal for potions relating to healing and resting. It is made in the same way as full moon water, but instead of a full moon, you let the light of a new moon shine on it.

Toil and Trouble

Make sure any water you use is safe and pollutant free. You can often get water tested for free or for a small fee at your local health department. Some townships, or other city government offices, also do testing. In addition, do-it-yourself testing kits are available at hardware stores.

If you have the collecting and storing capacity, you can save rainwater for your cleansing and potion needs. Before using collected rainwater, though, you might want to have it tested to make sure it hasn't picked up any kind of contaminants.

Potion Precautions

When preparing and using a potion, you need to take certain precautions. Following the same precautions and procedures every time you make a potion will also ensure that it works in the same manner time and time again. Some of the following precautions are quite obvious, while others you might not have considered before. All are equally important.

 Toil and Trouble

As a practitioner of magic, it is your responsibility to know exactly what it is you are working with. If you ever have a problem with your potion, such as an illness or allergic reaction, you must take responsibility for the problem. "I didn't know" is not a valid excuse.

The Intensity of Intent

I touched briefly on the concept of intent in Chapter 1. Intent is the most important ingredient in every potion you make. Intent is the reason why you are making the potion in the first place. Do you want to increase your self-esteem? Are you looking to relieve tension? Do you need money? Are you in need of a kick-start to your creativity? You must have a positive intent when preparing your potions, as you will incorporate those intentions into your potion making.

Which Way Is Your Energy Flowing?

While preparing any potion, you need to pour your own energy into your creation. This means having a clear and conscious mind while performing these magical workings. You transfer energy into the potion whether you want to or not, so make sure your energy is positive!

Because your energy flows into your potions when you make them, you shouldn't make potions when you are angry or upset. Your negative energy will transfer into the potion and it will not have the effects you wanted. I suggest keeping a calming potion such as a tea or an infusion (see Chapters 4 and 5 for recipes) on hand at all times. This way, if you do find yourself wanting to make a potion when you are upset, you can use the calming potion and give yourself a chance to mellow and rethink your position.

If, after making a potion, you realize that your intent was not clear, or your energy was negative, throw it out. Don't use it, and don't give it to anyone else. Just toss it and start over when you have positive intent and emotions.

Enchanting Explanations

Magic, spells, and potions can all be a lot of fun, but it's important to remember that it's also serious business. Although it might seem like there are a lot of precautions to remember, they are all here for your safety so that you will be able to enjoy your magic instead of dealing with unwanted consequences.

Sneezy, Wheezy, and Other Medical Problems

It is very important that you make sure you do not have any allergies to any of the ingredients you use. Always make sure to mark your jars, bottles, or other containers with a list of ingredients so you know what is in them.

Although many herbs are safe for consumption, some of these same herbs might not be safe with some preexisting medical conditions, including heart defects, liver problems, pregnancy, or breast-feeding. Always check with a doctor to make sure any herbal product you plan to take is safe for you to consume.

Cleansing Inside and Out

Make sure everything you use is clean, both physically and magically. This means that all tools should be washed with soap and water and then blessed through ritual.

 Concoction Clues

> Although it might be convenient to buy dried herbs in bulk—and by this I mean the type where you go into the store and scoop out the amount you want—it might not be very sanitary. You don't know who else has been sticking his or her hands into the same containers! If you're buying herbs, I recommend buying them prepackaged or fresh so that you can wash them yourself.

All herbs, fruits, and vegetables should also be washed, just as you would when preparing any other food. Similarly, all ingredients should also be blessed. An easy way to do this is to ask your patron deity or deities to bless them while you are soaking or rinsing them in water.

The Essence of Essential Oils

When working with essential oils, there are two main rules to keep in mind.

First, do not ingest essential oils—they are extremely potent, and you could do permanent damage to your body if you ingest them. Essential oils are the pure volatile oil removed from plant material.

Second, because of their extreme potency, pure essential oils should never be applied directly to the skin without being diluted first. This can be done with water or by adding a few drops to a non-toxic carrier oil such as grape seed oil, almond oil, or olive oil, just to name a few. Carrier oils are vegetable type oils that do not contain volatile oils. When using essential oils on a censer, only place a few drops of oil on it at a time to avoid steam burns. Never put your face into the smoke or steam—not only will it be hot, but the fumes might be overpowering.

The Least You Need to Know

- Magical tools can either be traditional or modern. No matter what kind you use, make sure they are physically and magically clean before use.

- In order to help keep their energy positive, your tools should only be used for magical and not mundane purposes.

- Always make sure you know your ingredients are safe for use.

- Precautions should always be taken when preparing potions to ensure the safety of the preparer and the user.

Chapter 3

Magical Uses of Plants

In This Chapter

- Adding plants to your potions
- Discovering the magical properties of plants

Plants have been used for their magical properties for centuries. No one knows for sure how plants were given these powers or even how humans discovered their uses. One theory claims the knowledge was passed on to exceptional humans chosen by faeries or even the Gods themselves. These humans were not only taught what plants to use for different types of ailments or wishes, but also which part of the plant to use. No matter how they were first discovered, practitioners over the centuries have relied heavily on the magical abilities—also known as correspondences—each plant has. Today, plants can be used in potions to harness their God-given powers.

The ingredients listed in this chapter are only some of the plant products you can use while experimenting with your potions. You will find them categorized by different plant parts believed to hold the greatest concentration of the particular magical ability. Unless you have an allergy or certain medical conditions, these ingredients are generally considered edible and can be used in your potable potions. There are many more you can use in your nonpotable potions! Entire books can be found which detail the magical properties of plants, and as your practice grows you will want to add some of these books to your library.

Use this chapter as your reference guide. You can come back to it whenever you need to plan a potion and its ingredients.

Bewitching Petals

Many flowers are edible, although some do have a bitter or strong taste. Flowers can either be dried or used fresh in your potions. You may use the actual petal chopped into small pieces and blended into your potion or you can make teas and other potions by the methods covered later in this chapter.

 Concoction Clues _____

> Always write down the ingredients you use in your potions. Not only is this necessary for safety reasons, but you need to know your ingredients if you want to make the potion again! If you don't like the way the potion worked out, you also know what not to do again.

Following is a list of some flowers you can use along with their magical correspondence.

Flower	Magical Benefits
Bee Balm	Induces sleep, love, success, and healing
Borage	Courage and psychic powers
Calendula	Comfort, health, and psychic dreams
Chamomile	Love, money, purification, and sleep
Chervil	Symbolizes new life and new beginnings
Clove (flower buds)	Protection, exorcism, love, and money
Clover	Protection, money, love, fidelity, exorcism, and success
Coltsfoot	Love and visions
Heather	Protection, rain making, and luck
Jasmine	Love, money, and prophetic dreams
Lavender	Love, protection, sleep, chastity, longevity, purification, happiness, and peace
Linden	Protection, immortality, luck, love, and sleep
Mullein	Courage, protection, health, love, divination, and exorcism
Pansy	Love, rain magic, and divination
Primrose	Protection and love
Rose	Love, psychic powers, healing, divination, luck and protection
Violets	Protection, luck, love, lust, wishes, peace and healing

continues

continued

Flower	Magical Benefits
Yarrow	Courage, love, psychic powers, and exorcism
Ylang-Ylang	Love, lust, sex, and peace

Toil and Trouble

Chamomile is part of the ragweed family, a common group of allergens. If you are allergic to ragweed, you might be allergic to chamomile as well.

Too much pansy can cause skin problems.

Spellbinding Leaves

The leaves of herbs and plants have a wide variety of tastes, many of which you are probably already familiar with. Leaves can either be dried or used fresh in your potions. You may use the actual leaf chopped into small pieces and blended into your potion or you can make teas and other potions by the methods covered later on in this chapter.

Don't be afraid to combine different leaves and herbs to give your potions a unique flavor. Experiment to find tastes and scents that you like.

Toil and Trouble

Many herbs can also be found in essential oil form, but you should *never use them* in your potable potions. However, adding a few drops of essential oils to your nonpotable potions gives them a wonderful scent and adds the desired magical correspondences.

Following is a list of some leaves you can use along with their magical correspondence.

Leaf	Magical Benefits
Alfalfa	Prosperity, anti-hunger, and money
Aloe (peel leaves for internal use)	Protection and luck
Amaranth	Healing, protection, and invisibility
Basil	Love, exorcism, wealth, and protection
Bedstraw	Love
Birch (must be fresh young leaves)	Protection, exorcism, and purification
Blackberry	Healing, money, and protection
Bone Set	Protection and exorcism
Borage	Courage and psychic powers
Burdock	Protection and healing
Cabbage	Luck

continues

continued

Leaf	Magical Benefits
Calendula	Comfort, dreams, and psychic dreams
Catnip	Cat magic (for use with *familiars*), love, beauty, and happiness
Celandine	Protection, escape, happiness, and legal matters
Coltsfoot	Love and visions
Columbine	Courage and love
Dill	Protection, money, lust, and luck
Endive	Lust and love
Eucalyptus	Healing and protection
Feverfew	Protection
Goldenrod	Money and divination
Henna	Healing
Holly (berries are poisonous)	Protection, anti-lightning, luck, and dream magic
Houseleek	Luck, protection, and love
Hyssop*	Purification and protection
Irish Moss	Money, luck, and protection
Lady's Mantle	Love
Larch (needles)	Protection and anti-theft
Lavender	Love, protection, sleep, chastity, longevity, purification, happiness, and peace
Lemon Balm	Love, success, and healing
Lettuce	Chastity, protection, love, divination, and sleep
Loosestrife	Peace and protection
Marjoram	Protection, love, happiness, health, and money

Leaf	Magical Benefits
Meadowsweet	Love, divination, peace, and happiness
Mint	Money, love, lust, healing, exorcism, travel, and protection
Mugwort*	Strength, psychic powers, protection, prophetic dreams, healing, and astral projection
Mullein	Courage, protection, health, love, divination, and exorcism
Parsley	Love, protection, and purification
Pennyroyal	Strength, protection, and peace
Periwinkle	Love, lust, mental powers, money, and protection
Plantain	Healing, protection, strength, and snake repelling
Raspberry	Protection and love
Sage*	Immortality, longevity, wisdom, protection, and wishes
St. John's Wort	Health, power, protection, strength, love, divination, and happiness
Savory	Mental powers
Senna	Love
Scullcap	Love, fidelity, and peace
Thyme	Health, healing, sleep, psychic powers, love, purification, and courage
Wintergreen	Protection, healing, and hex breaking
Witch Grass	Happiness, love, lust, and exorcism
Yerba Santa	Beauty, healing, psychic powers, and protection

*Do not use excessively or for an extended period of time

Concoction Clues

Sage is often burned for its protective and purifying qualities. The proper type of sage to use for this is white sage.

Many potions are made with herbs, which can be quite expensive if purchased from the store. You can save money by growing your own. Most herbs are very easy to grow, and they don't have to take up a lot of room. Even a small apartment has room for a few planters on a windowsill.

Mystical Roots, Rootstock, and Bulbs

When using most roots and *rootstock* in your potions, you must first boil them, and then add the infused water to your potions. Bulbs can generally be cut into pieces, cooked, and mashed and then added to your potions. Some roots, such as carrots, can be prepared the same way as bulbs.

Magical Definitions

A **rootstock** is another name for a rhizome, the underground stem of a plant from which roots grow.

Following is a list of some common roots (identified by an R), rootstock (RS), and bulbs (B) you can use, along with their magical correspondence.

Root, Root-stock, Bulb	Magical Benefits
Angelica (R, RS)	Exorcism, protection, healing, and visions
Beet (B)	Love
Blue Flag (RS)	Money
Burdock (R)	Protection and healing
Carrot (R)	Fertility and lust
Chicory (RS)	Removing obstacles, invisibility, and favors
Comfrey (RS)	Safety during travel and money
Cyclamen (RS)	Fertility, protection, happiness, and lust
Echinacea (RS)	Strengthening spells
Elecampane (RS)	Love, protection, and psychic powers
Galangal (RS)	Protection, lust, health, money, psychic powers, and hex breaking
Garlic (B)	Protection, healing, lust, anti-theft, and exorcism
Ginger (RS)	Love, money, success, and power
Ginseng (R)	Love, wishes, healing, beauty, protection, and lust
Leek (B)	Love, protection, and exorcism
Licorice (RS)	Love, lust, and fidelity
Lovage (RS)	Love
Onion (B)	Protection, exorcism, healing, money, prophetic dreams, and lust
Orris Root (RS)	Love, protection, and divination
Radish (B)	Protection and lust

continues

continued

Root, Root-stock, Bulb	Magical Benefits
Sarsaparilla (RS)	Love and money
Solomon's Seal (RS)	Protection and exorcism
Spikenard (RS, R)	Love
Turnip (B)	Protection and ending relationships

Mesmerizing Wood, Stems, and Bark

When using wood and bark, you must boil the wood or bark and then use the infused water for your potions. Stems can generally be put through a juicer or cut into pieces, cooked, and mashed and then added directly to your potions.

Following is a list of some wood (W), stems (S), and bark (B) you can use, along with their magical correspondence.

Wood, Stem, Bark	Magical Properties
Birch (B)	Protection, exorcism, and purification
Celery (S)	Mental powers, lust, and psychic powers
Dogwood (dried bark)	Wishes and protection
Elm (bark of young branches)	Love

Wood, Stem, Bark	Magical Properties
Larch (B)	Protection and anti-theft
Magnolia (B)	Fidelity
Myrrh *(Resin)*	Protection, exorcism, healing, and spirituality
Oak (B)	Protection, health, money, healing, potency, fertility, and luck
Poplar (B)	Money
Rhubarb (S)	Protection and fidelity
Sandalwood (W)	Protection, healing, exorcism, and spirituality
Sassafras (B)	Health and money
Willow (B)	Love, divination, protection, and healing

Magical Definitions

Resins are the hard (or semi-hard) deposits left by plant sap. Resins are not water soluble, and should be used in tinctures.

Enchanting Seeds, Grains, Fruits, and Nuts

When adding most seeds, grains, and nuts to your potions, you need to grind them before use. Afterward, you can either add the powder to your potions, boil it in water to thin it, or mix it with herbs to use as a tea. Fruits can either be thrown into a food processor to liquefy them (be sure to remove the pulp), or processed in a juicer.

Following is a list of seeds (S), grains (G), fruits (F), and nuts (N) you might consider using in your potions, along with their magical correspondence.

Toil and Trouble _____

Nuts are a very common allergen and can cause anaphylactic shock. Be sure neither you nor anyone else using your potions made with nuts has any nut allergies. You should also use separate tools (such as a grinder) when working with nuts, so as to not pass on trace oils to anyone with an allergy to them.

Seeds, Grain, Fruit, or Nut	Magical Benefits
Allspice (dried berry of the pimento) (F)	Money, luck, and healing
Almonds (N)	Money, prosperity, and wisdom
Angelica (S)	Exorcism, protection, healing, and visions
Anise (S)	Youth, protection, and purification
Apple (F)	Love, healing, garden magic, and immortality
Apricot (F)	Love
Avocado (F)	Love, lust, and beauty

Seeds, Grain, Fruit, or Nut	Magical Benefits
Barley (G)	Love, healing, and protection
Banana (F)	Fertility, potency, and prosperity
Blackberry (F)	Healing, money, and protection
Blueberry (F)	Protection
Brazil Nut (N)	Love
Burdock (S)	Protection and healing
Caraway (S)	Protection, lust, health, anti-theft, and mental powers
Carob (F)	Protection and health
Cardamom (S)	Lust and love
Cashew (N)	Money
Cherry (F)	Love and divination
Chestnut (N)	Love
Coconut (F)	Purification, protection, and chastity
Coriander (S)	Love, health, and healing
Corn (S)	Protection, luck, and divination
Cubeb (unripe berries) (F)	Love
Cucumber (F)	Chastity, healing, and fertility
Dill (S)	Protection, money, lust, and luck
Elder Berries (cooked)	Protection, healing, prosperity, and sleep
Fennel (S)	Protection, healing, and purification
Fenugreek (S)	Money
Fig (F)	Divination, fertility, and love
Flax (S)	Money, protection, beauty, psychic powers, and healing

continues

continued

Seeds, Grain, Fruit, or Nut	Magical Benefits
Grape (F)	Fertility, garden magic, mental powers, and money
Hops (F)	Healing and sleep
Juniper Berries (F)	Protection, anti-theft, love, exorcism, and health
Lemon (F)	Longevity, purification, love and friendship
Mulberry (F)	Protection and strength
Mustard (S)	Fertility, protection, and mental powers
Oats (G)	Money
Olive (F)	Healing, peace, fertility, potency, protection, and lust
Orange (F)	Love, divination, luck, and money
Papaya (F)	Love and protection
Pea (S)	Money and love
Peach (F)	Love, exorcism, longevity, fertility, and wishes
Pear (F)	Lust and love
Pecan (N)	Money and employment
Pineapple (F)	Luck, money, and chastity
Pistachio (N)	Breaking love spells
Plum (F)	Healing
Pomegranate (F)	Divination, luck, wishes, wealth, and fertility
Pumpkin (F)	Prosperity and abundance
Raspberry (F)	Protection and love

Seeds, Grain, Fruit, or Nut	Magical Benefits
Rowan (F)	Psychic powers, healing, protection, power, and success
Strawberry (F)	Love and luck
Sunflower (S)	Fertility, wishes, health, and wisdom
Walnut (S)	Health, mental powers, infertility, and wishes

 Concoction Clues

For a clean and happy home, make a cleansing potion by adding 1 cup vinegar and 1 cup lemon juice to 2 gallons of water. Use on floors, counters, windows, and appliances to rid your house of any negativity.

Never cast a love spell on a particular person, as this interferes with his or her free will. Instead, love spells should be designed to bring a person who has the qualities you are looking for into your life. Keep in mind, of course, that there is always the chance that you are looking for the wrong qualities.

The Least You Need to Know

- Although we don't know where the knowledge of plant magic originally came from, for centuries people all over the world have agreed on their powers.

- Different plants have different magical attributes. By using these plants in your potions you bring these attributes into your life.

- Each plant has a specific part that holds the essence of the attribute stronger than the other parts.

- It's extremely important to know what you are allergic to before you begin working with any plant material.

Chapter 4

Tempting Teas

In This Chapter

- Using tea potions
- Choosing and preparing ingredients
- Storing your tea mixtures
- Getting started with some recipes

Teas are great potions for beginners; not only are they one of the easiest potions to make, you can really let your creative juices flow when putting them together. Depending on the recipe, the prep work can be time consuming, but in just a short time you'll be making all kinds of new magical and flavorful elixirs.

An Easy Elixir

Teas have been around for thousands of years, and they have never gone out of style. The simple process of making and drinking teas is an enjoyable experience.

Mix, Steep, and Experience

Mix, *steep*, and experience—this is the easiest way
to understand the process of making and using
teas. You simply combine the ingredients, let them
steep in hot water, and then experience the potion
as it radiates throughout your body and performs
its magic.

Magical Definitions

The process of turning dried herbs into
a tea is called **steeping**. When you steep
the herbs, you soak the plant material in
liquid to move the plant's essence from the
plant into the liquid.

But Why Tea?

Teas work in two main ways. First of all, when you
drink tea, with every swallow you imbibe whatever
magical qualities are in the brew. Because the base
of tea is water, it moves very quickly through your
body and is easily absorbed into your system. You
become one with the tea, one with the magic. The
magic becomes a part of you. Tea also has aromatherapy qualities. As you sit to drink your tea,
take the time to savor its aroma. Breathe in the
scent and feel it becoming a part of you.

Add a Little Atmosphere

Before sitting down with your tea, create an atmosphere appropriate to you tea's meaning. Light

colored candles with corresponding qualities (see Appendix B). Use symbols or pictures to represent what you are wishing for. You might even want to play music that relates to the magical work you are performing or that puts you in a meditative mood. The atmosphere helps to get you into the right frame of mind and deepens your focus to the task at hand.

Toil and Trouble

Make sure your atmosphere reflects the qualities you are looking for and is safe. For example, if you just need to relax, a candle is fine, but if you plan on going to sleep (or think you could accidentally fall asleep!), pass on lighting a candle, just to be on the safe side.

Take your time when drinking your tea—this isn't something to be rushed. Turn off the TV, unplug the phone, put the dog in another room, and try to avoid any other distractions.

So Many Herbs, So Little Time

Probably the hardest part about making a tea is deciding what to put in it, because there are dozens of herbs and plants you can choose from.

Finding Your Focus

Begin by focusing on your intent and then narrowing down the field of available plants and herbs to those that correspond with your intent.

Use the list in Chapter 3 to find different herbs and plants you can use that fit with your focus. This will eliminate a lot of herbs, but you might still be left with a number to choose from.

What Do Your Taste Buds Have to Say?

You can eliminate more choices by getting rid of anything with a scent or taste you are not terribly fond of. I recommend taking a day and taste testing different herbs. Because this can be a big undertaking, spend one day just working on whether or not you like the taste or smell. If you don't like the taste of something, you probably aren't going to want to use it in any of your potable potions! Keep a list of herbs that you like and don't like so you have an easy guide to refer to.

 Concoction Clues

Although many of your teas will taste wonderful, some will be bitter or strong. This doesn't mean they are any less powerful, just different. Try adding sweeteners such as honey to help improve the taste.

After you've sorted herbs into "yummy" and "yuck" categories, you can begin working on blending them to come up with flavor combinations. Be prepared for some trial and error. But don't worry—if you don't feel like experimenting on your own, you can try some of the basic recipes at the end of this chapter.

Savor the Flavor

If you haven't made your own teas before, I suggest starting with just two or three different herbs. As you become more practiced and familiar with the tastes of the herbs and how they complement one another, you can experiment by combining more kinds together.

Not only do you need to experiment with the types of herbs you use, but also the amounts. In a calming tea you might want to use lavender and bergamot. You can mix equal amounts of these two herbs, or try one part lavender to two parts bergamot, or vice versa. If you like the flavor of one herb more than another, add a little more of it to your mixture. Remember that it's your potion, and you get to make the rules!

Always make sure you measure out your amounts and write everything down. If you end up loving a particular blend, you'll want to know how you made it! Keep a journal of the combinations you have tried with a note on whether you liked it or not.

This is just as important for teas you don't care for as it is for teas you do. If you make a tea and don't like it, you don't want to make the same one again by mistake!

 **Concoction Clues**

When you are first trying a tea, only make a small amount—use measuring spoons instead of cups as your "parts." If you don't like the tea or were not satisfied with the results, very little will have gone to waste, and if you are happy with tea, it won't be difficult to make more in a larger quantity.

Mix It Up

The first step in the physical preparation of your teas is to combine dried plant material to create the mixture you want. You can do this ahead of time so you always have some on hand.

Actually, I recommend setting aside a day when you are in the mood to do some magical work and making up a variety of tea mixtures to store for later use. Make teas you know you will use often, such as those for sleep, calmness, and relaxation; maintaining good health; and healing.

You should only use dried herbs in your teas, not fresh. If you grow herbs yourself, you will need to dry them and crush them just a little bit, but not too finely, before adding them to your preparations.

If you use an electric grinder, you will only need to pulse it a couple of times to get the desired effect.

Measure each ingredient into a bowl large enough to hold your tea mixture. Mix the ingredients very thoroughly, and then store with one of the methods we will go over a little later in this chapter.

No Boiling Required

The water you use should be hot, but not boiling. (Boiling water makes bitter tea.) Let boiling water cool off for a few minutes before pouring it over tea leaves.

Allow the tea to steep in hot water for three to five minutes. You can use a tea ball to hold the ingredients or make actual bags for your teas. Personally, I find tea balls work just as well as tea bags, and they are a lot less time consuming.

Although I don't like to do this, I know some people who simply throw the dried ingredients into a cup and pour water over it, letting the herbs float around loose.

 Concoction Clues

If you want to use a sweetener—artificial sweeteners, sugar, or honey—add it after the tea has steeped. I recommend honey, especially if you can buy it fresh, as it keeps with the natural nature of your tea.

Concoction Clues

Take advantage of the power of the sun by making sun tea. Simply place some tea mixture (in bags, tea balls, or loose) into a clear jar or pitcher with a lid, add water, seal the lid, and let the mixture sit in the sun for several hours. You can then refrigerate the container for iced tea on hot days.

Experience the Feeling

Finally, you get to the best part! Sit back, relax, and sip your tea. While drinking, meditate on what it is you want the tea to do for you. Notice the feel of the tea on your taste buds and in your mouth.

 Concoction Clues

If you are new to visualizing or meditating, you can make yourself an audiotape to play and walk yourself through the process when you are ready. Tell yourself how you want to feel and what you want to pay attention to. Make a list of points you want to make sure you don't miss while meditating. Having audio prompts makes meditating far easier than breaking concentration by trying to read instructions.

In your mind, follow the tea down your esophagus and into your stomach. Feel the tea branching throughout your body as it releases its magic into your system. As you meditate, visualize yourself acquiring the desired quality or action the tea was made to enhance. Imagine yourself already in the condition the tea is made to bring about. Concentrating on the desired effect as you drink your tea potion adds a great deal of positive energy to your magical workings and significantly increases the power to make your wishes and dreams come true.

Where to Put It All

Now that you have defined your intent, chosen your herbs, mixed them all up, and have them sitting in a bowl on your kitchen counter, it's time to decide how to store your tea blends for later use.

Bagging It

You can purchase tea bag paper (you can find it either in sheets or prefolded) and fill your own bags. Unless you purchased sealable bags, you will need a stapler to hold the bags shut. Measure enough of the dry mixture and pour it into a bag, fold it closed and staple shut. I use about a tablespoon of dried mix per cup; use less for a weaker tea, more for a stronger tea.

You can even add a string attached to a small piece of paper to identify the type of tea it is—just like store-bought tea bags. You should always label your tea before you give it (or sell it) to someone else , although if you will be the only one using the teas, labeling it isn't necessary.

 **Concoction Clues** _____

> Storing filled tea bags in a resealable plastic storage bag will keep your tea fresher longer. No matter how you store your teas, try to keep as much air out of them as possible. If you use jars, throw some cheesecloth or wax paper inside of the jar to take up air space.

Jar It Up

Canning type jars, or other jars with screw-on lids, work just as well as tea bags for storing your blends. Mark each jar with the type of tea and ingredients. Get creative and give them descriptive, yet interesting, names.

Tea blends should be stored in a dark and cool location to help keep the herbs fresh and full of flavor.

Zip It Up

Food storage bags, especially those with zip-lock seals, are also excellent for storing your mixtures. The benefit of the bags is you can squeeze air out after each use, before you reseal the bag. The less contact the dry mixture has with air, the longer the herbs will stay fresh and flavorful.

Bags of any kind should also be stored in a dark, cool location.

Keep Refrigerated

Teas that have already been prepared with water can be stored in the refrigerator to keep them fresh. With no preservatives, however, don't keep brewed teas for more than a week.

 Concoction Clues

> If you want to keep teas longer, you can freeze them. Try pouring a tea into ice cube trays. Then when you want iced tea, fill a glass with cubes and a little water to get them to melt. You can microwave a cup of ice cubes for a hot tea.

Let's Get Started

Here are come recipes to get you started on your tea brewing practices. Feel free to experiment with these teas by altering the amounts of each ingredient you use.

Find True Love Tea

Use this tea to help you find your true love. When preparing and drinking the tea, you should focus on the qualities you want your true love to have, not a specific person. You can also focus on the attributes you want others to notice in you.

2 parts lemon balm leaves

2 parts mint leaves

1 part catnip leaves

1 part chamomile flowers

1 part clover flowers

1 part yarrow flowers

Keep Me Healthy Tea

Prepare this tea when you are already in good
health and want to maintain it. As you drink it,
visualize yourself in the days to come as healthy,
happy, and active.

4 parts calendula flowers

1 part mullein leaves or flowers

1 part marjoram leaves

1 part St. John's Wort

Heal Me Tea

Although your potions should never replace a trip
to the doctor when you are ill, this tea can give you
a magical boost to speed your healing. Focus on
ridding your body of whatever ails you. If you are
running a fever, add 1 part of feverfew.

4 parts rose petals

3 parts violet petals

2 parts dried apples

1 part dried blackberries

1 part eucalyptus leaves

1 part ginseng root

Sip for Success Tea

While sipping this tea, envision yourself succeeding at a current project you are undertaking. Use tangible images such as seeing the project complete. Feel yourself doing your job successfully. This tea works best when working with specific projects or situations. Don't just imagine yourself being successful—define what success means to you.

4 parts clover flowers

2 parts lemon balm leaves

1 part ginger root

Keep Me Safe Protection Tea

This tea is to protect you from psychic attacks from others. As you drink this, imagine yourself surrounded by a giant protective bubble of white light. Think of the bubble as a protective shield that keeps anything out that can harm you and lets only love and light through. Feel the strength in knowing you are safe and protected.

4 parts thyme leaves

2 parts sage leaves

1 part basil leaves

1 part clover flowers

a pinch of mugwort

Home Protection Tea

Slowly sip this tea as you walk throughout your home, both inside and outside if possible. Walk along each wall and your property line as you outline your living area. The aroma will surround your home with protection while the tea flows through your body and radiates into the environment around you.

> 3 parts mint leaves
>
> 2 parts raspberry leaves
>
> 1 part eucalyptus leaves
>
> 1 part rose petals
>
> 1 part lavender flowers
>
> a pinch of irish moss

Psychic Kick Tea

This tea is to help you increase your psychic abilities; sip it slowly while meditating before performing any type of psychic task such as dream interpretations, scrying (a form of divination where the reader looks into a reflective surface such as water), or readings. Note that this tea is not meant to be used on a daily basis, just when the need arises.

> 3 parts thyme leaves
>
> 3 parts rose petals
>
> 3 parts yarrow flowers
>
> a pinch of St. John's Wort
>
> a pinch of mugwort

Courage and Strength Tea

Use this tea when you need an extra boost of
strength and courage. Visualize yourself as being
the strong and courageous person you will need to
be in order to overcome the situation. Imagine
your problems shrinking in size until you tower
over them and see them as small and insignificant.

3 parts pennyroyal leaves

1 part thyme leaves

1 part columbine leaves

1 part borage flowers (or leaves)

1 part mullein flowers

Calming Peace Tea

This tea is for when you are completely stressed out
and need desperately to unwind, calm down, and
relax. Try sipping it sitting under the shade of a tree
or in a warm, relaxing bubble bath. Visualize yourself at complete ease. While sipping this tea, use
other relaxation techniques, such as deep breathing,
to help it work to its fullest potential. Be careful
though, this tea tends to make the user very sleepy.

4 parts lavender flowers

3 parts violet flowers

2 parts calendula flowers

1 part pennyroyal leaves

1 part meadowsweet leaves

a pinch of skull cap leaves

Show Me the Money Tea

This tea is designed to help you attract money. Don't expect money to simply fall into your lap after drinking this tea; however, it will increase your chances of having monetary opportunities present themselves. If you feel a strong desire to buy a lottery ticket after drinking this tea, by all means do so.

> 4 parts mint leaves
>
> 3 parts alfalfa leaves
>
> 1 part irish moss
>
> 1 part clover flowers
>
> 1 part chamomile flowers

A Good Night's Sleep Tea

Drink this tea up to an hour before going to bed for a great night of peaceful sleep. You will awaken in the morning feeling renewed and refreshed.

> 4 parts chamomile flowers
>
> 3 parts lavender flowers
>
> ½ part thyme leaves

Hip Hip Huzzah Tea

This tea is for when you are down and out and need a bit of cheering up. Designed to lift your mood and spirits, sip this tea while remembering a happy occasion in your life. Imagine yourself back at that moment and bring that feeling back to the present with you.

> 4 parts marjoram leaves
>
> 3 parts catnip leaves
>
> 2 parts St. John's Wort leaves
>
> 1 part violet flowers
>
> 1 part lavender flowers
>
> 1 part witch grass

The Least You Need to Know

- Prepare your teas ahead of time so they are ready when needed.

- When you drink a tea potion, your body absorbs the potion's magic, making it radiate from you.

- Always use *dried* (rather than fresh) plant material to make your tea.

- Storing dried tea blends is easy and convenient; however, remember to keep tea in a cool, dark place with as little air contact as possible.

Indispensable Infusions

In This Chapter

- Using infusions
- Choosing and preparing ingredients
- Storing your infusions
- Getting started with some recipes

Infusions can be made with water or various kinds of oils. In this chapter, I limit my discussion to water-based infusions. Chapter 6 delves into infusions made with oil.

Infusion Insights

The preparation for *infusions* is very similar to teas, with one major difference: whereas teas should never be boiled, infusions require boiling water. You can think of an infusion as similar to a highly concentrated tea. Infusions are more potent than teas because more of the plants' essences are transferred to the water through the boiling process.

Their potency makes infusions more suited for external use rather than for internal use, although water-based infusions can be drunk as long as they are made with ingredients that are safe for human consumption.

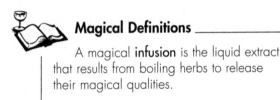

Magical Definitions

A magical **infusion** is the liquid extract that results from boiling herbs to release their magical qualities.

Soak It In

Infusions are excellent for use in baths, foot soaks, hand soaks, body splashes, or poultices.

An infusion is jammed-packed with the essence and magic from the materials you use to make it. As you use the infusion, that magic and essence radiates into your skin and the air around you, wrapping you in a magical cocoon.

Concoction Clues

When using an infusion as a foot soak, add 1 cup of the infusion to each quart of water. For baths, pour 1 gallon into a full tub.

Soaking infusions also have an aromatherapy quality. As you soak, take deep breaths and inhale the scents from the infusion, bringing the magic deeper into yourself.

Infusions can also be used like liquid cleansers. Soaking or rinsing items in the infusion transfers the magical properties from the infusion to the item.

You can use infusions to wipe down walls and counters, clean mirrors, and mop floors to fill a room with the desired energy.

Toil and Trouble

Before using any infusion on furniture or walls, test a small area first to see if any ingredients in the infusion will leave a stain. You can weaken the coloring agents by adding more water to your infusion.

Set the Mood

No matter how you use your infusion, you should take care to set a mood that matches your intent. Let your environment reflect the magic you want to create. Light candles, play music, and now that you know how to create your own teas (see Chapter 4), why not have a cup that corresponds with your magical workings?

Concoction Clues _____

> As you learn to make more types of potions, begin adding them to your magical practices. You can soak in an infusion while drinking a cup of tea and finish up with an infusion body splash or a magical lotion. By using multiple potions, you increase your energy and focus, helping to bring your wishes into reality.

While using your infusions, meditate on the task at hand, bringing your wishes and hopes into sharp focus. If you've prepared a meditation how-to audiotape (refer to Chapter 4), use it with your infusion to help you concentrate and center.

Infusion Preparation

The first steps of preparing an infusion are very similar to those of preparing a tea. The differences begin with the actual cooking or heating of the infusion.

Infuse Your Infusions

Begin your infusion preparation by establishing your intent. When making infusions you can use any safe plant material, whether fresh or dried, including roots, herbs, fruits, bark, and resins. If you plan on drinking your infusion, however, make sure that your ingredients are safe for consumption.

Refer to Chapter 3 for a list of potential ingredients. Narrow down your list by removing any allergens or items with a scent you just plain don't like. If you don't plan on drinking your infusion, you won't have to worry about taste, but can instead concern yourself with the fragrances you create by combining different herbs together. When taste isn't a factor, you have a lot more options for the infusions you create.

Blend Your Bounty

As with teas, you can mix up ingredients to use for your infusions ahead of time so they are handy when you need them. Again, take a day when you are in a particularly magical mood and have the supplies to make up batches of dried ingredients. Mix batches of infusions you know you will use frequently.

 Concoction Clues _____

> Food processors come in quite handy when mixing up large batches of dried material for infusions. They insure proper mixing and, on a chopping setting, break down larger ingredients to a more manageable size, giving you more room for water in your pot or cauldron.

Turn Up the Heat

When you are ready to prepare the actual infusion, put the dried material in a pot of water. (If possible, use full moon water for extra energy.) You can either tie up the ingredients in some cheesecloth or just let them float loose. The more ingredients you use, the more potent your infusion will be. Allow for plenty of water, as you will be boiling your infusion for a while and some of the water will evaporate.

Set your pot on the stove and turn it on high. Let the mixture come to a full rolling boil and then let simmer for a half an hour. Remove the pot from heat and let the infusion sit for a while to cool off.

If you have placed the herbs in cheesecloth, after the water has cooled enough, wring out the cheese-cloth over the infusion. If the mix is floating loosely, use a screen strainer to remove it from the water. Your infusion is now ready to be used or stored.

Pack It Up

How you store your infusions depends in large part on whether you are storing dry ingredients or the actual infusion.

Keeping It Dry

The dry ingredients for infusions can be stored in much the same was as the ingredients for teas (see Chapter 4). You can store them in food storage bags, screw-top jars, or any other airtight containers. Keep in mind, though, that infusions use larger amounts of ingredients than teas do, so you will need large containers to store dry ingredients.

I occasionally buy some foods in bulk and have saved gallon-size pickle jars and giant plastic pretzel barrels. Their large mouths make them easy to fill and scoop out herbs. Best of all, they don't cost extra. Large plastic ice cream tubs are also ideal, or pick up some inexpensive plastic storage bins. You can usually find these really cheap after holidays.

 Toil and Trouble

Occasionally, you might find that some of your herbs have molded, an especially common problem in areas of high humidity. Do not use molded herbs in any magical potion, as mold is a strong allergen. You can compost any herbs that have gone bad, or simply bury them.

Wrap It Up

You can store your mixtures loose, or tie them up with twine in cheesecloth, muslin, or some other soft, porous material so all you have to do is drop it into the pot of water when you're ready to make an infusion. Cheesecloth or other material bags should also be stored in some kind of sealed container, such as a zip-lock plastic bag, to help keep the ingredients fresh.

Chill Out

The final liquid infusion can be refrigerated in jars or pitchers. Save old milk or juice cartons (be sure to wash them out thoroughly) to store large amounts of infusions.

Potable infusions should only be stored for a few days in the fridge. If you aren't planning to drink your infusion, you can keep it refrigerated for quite a while longer. If you notice it getting too cloudy or moldy however, pour it out on the ground outside. Magical concoctions should go back to the earth and not down a manmade drain unless they are being used in the bathtub. The earth will know what to do with it!

 Concoction Clues _____

> If you use a clear bottle to store your infusions, you can tell at a glance if the infusion is getting cloudy or moldy. When an infusion goes bad, mold will begin floating on the top of the liquid.

Infusion-sicles

Infusions can also be frozen either in ice cube trays or other freezer-proof plastic containers. Make sure you don't fill containers all the way to the top so the water has room to expand as it freezes. If you have a large freezer, this is an ideal way to store your infusions.

When you are ready to use the infusion, simply melt it and warm it up in a microwave, on your stove top, or set it outside on a warm day.

You can even throw infusion ice cubes into a hot bath. As they melt, they will release their properties into the water.

 Concoction Clues _____

> Freezing prepared infusions is the smartest and safest way to store your infusions. Frozen infusions do not mold or go bad and can be stored for long periods of time.

Let's Get Started

Try these recipes to get yourself started in your infusion creating practices. Experiment with them, making changes where you see fit. These recipes are quite powerful and potent, as well as rather elaborate. You can eliminate some of the ingredients to make them easier to create, which will also slightly reduce the infusion's potency. When it comes to infusions, anything goes!

Monday Morning Motivating Splash

Use this body splash on Monday morning, or any other time you need an extra bit of motivation. Simply splash it on after your bath or shower and let it air dry. Meditate on having the motivation to make it through the day or to get through any kind of problem you are having.

> 1 cup yarrow flowers
>
> 1 cup heather flowers
>
> 1 cup rose flowers
>
> 1 cup bergamot leaves
>
> ¼ cup chicory root
>
> ¼ cup lemon peel
>
> ¼ cup lime peel
>
> ¼ cup orange peel
>
> ¼ cup peppermint leaves
>
> 4 cloves

Muscle Relaxer Soak

Add this soak to your bath when your muscles are tense and you need to wind down. Visualize each muscle in your body relaxing. Use deep breathing relaxation techniques to help unwind.

> 3 cups cedar bark
>
> 3 cups lavender flowers
>
> 1 cup lemongrass

Purification Soak

This infusion should be added to your cleansing bath when preparing for a ritual. Meditate on purifying your thoughts and opening your mind to prepare for your ritual.

You can also use this infusion for cleaning or purifying rooms or objects. Simply set the items in the
infusion or use a sponge soaked in the infusion to
wipe areas down.

> 2 cups chamomile flowers
>
> 1 cup clover flowers
>
> ¼ cup pansy flowers
>
> 2 cups lavender flowers
>
> ¼ cup hyssop leaves
>
> ¼ cup thyme leaves
>
> 1 tsp anise
>
> ¼ cup lemon peel

Business Success Infusion

Use this infusion either as a soak added to your
bath, or soak a washcloth with it and lay it across
your forehead while you meditate on being successful in your work life. Try to focus on a specific
event or project instead of on a general feeling.

If possible, use this infusion at your work. Try wip-
ing down your desk with it, sprinkle droplets on
the floor, or water plants in your work area with
it—as they grow they will release the magic into
the air.

> 1 cup magnolia blossoms
>
> 1 cup chamomile blossoms
>
> ½ cup Balm of Gilead
>
> 1 cup bergamot leaves

½ cup tangerine peel

½ cup sage leaves

¼ cup peeled ginger root

3 cinnamon sticks

½ cup basil leaves

1 TB. juniper berries

Love Attraction Infusion

This infusion is designed to help you find your true love. While using this infusion, meditate on the qualities you want your true love to have. Do not visualize a specific person, as this interferes with his or her free will.

½ cup chamomile flowers

½ cup clover flowers

½ cup lavender flowers

½ cup jasmine flowers

½ cup primrose flowers

½ cup red rose petals

½ cup violet flowers

3 fresh basil leaves

1 TB. mint leaves

1 TB. raspberry leaves

1 inch peeled ginger root

1 small apple, peeled, cored, and sliced

Money Attraction Infusion

This infusion will help open your eyes to money-making opportunities. When using this infusion, visualize yourself receiving the money you need—but don't be greedy, and remember that needs and wants are two different things.

You can use this infusion in a bath or place a few drops at a time onto a lit charcoal tablet. The steam will release your magic into the world.

> ½ cup crushed pineapple chunks
>
> 1 pear peeled and sliced
>
> ½ cup oats
>
> ½ cup sassafras bark
>
> 1 inch ginger, peeled and sliced
>
> ½ cup flax seeds
>
> ½ cup cashews
>
> 1 chunk (about ¼ cup size) of oak bark

Healing Juice Soak

Add this infusion to a warm bath when you need some extra healing energy. Visualize whatever ails you leaving your body. Imagine your illness is being pulled out of you and into the water. Watch as you pull the plug and see your illness go down the drain.

If you are up to it, use this infusion to wipe down counters, toilets, sinks, doorknobs, and other places where germs congregate.

¼ cup rowan berries

¼ cup sunflower seeds

¼ cup elder berries

1 TB. fennel seeds

6 green olives

1 TB. coriander seeds

1 fresh cucumber, peeled and sliced

1 chunk willow bark

1 TB. angelica seeds

2 large fresh apples, peeled and sliced

5 chunks myrrh resin

I See Divination Infusion

Use this infusion either in your bath or soak a washcloth with it and lay it across your forehead before you begin any divination workings. Relax and focus on opening your mind to receive messages from the other side or your higher self.

While doing your divination work, drop a couple of drops at a time on a lit charcoal tablet, releasing the infusion into the air.

½ cup borage flowers

½ cup calendula flowers

5 cloves

¼ cup coltsfoot leaves or flowers

¼ cup jasmine flowers

¼ cup mullein flowers

¼ cup pansy flowers

½ cup rose petals

¼ cup yarrow flowers

¼ cup goldenrod leaves

½ cup shredded lettuce

Protection Infusion

Use this infusion to protect you from psychic attacks from others. As you soak in this protection infusion, imagine yourself surrounded by a giant protective bubble of white light. The bubble keeps anything out that can harm you and lets only love and light through. Feel the strength in knowing you are safe and protected.

To protect your home, fill a gallon pitcher with this infusion and walk around the outside of your home, pouring a line of the liquid all the way around the house.

¼ cup raspberries

¼ cup rowan berries

¼ cup mulberries

1 papaya, peeled and diced

1 cup coconut flakes

1 chunk dogwood bark

3 chunks of myrrh resin

1 tsp. burdock root, chopped

1 tsp. ginseng root, chopped

1 tsp. St. John's Wort

Get a Job Infusion

This infusion is designed to help you find the perfect job. Use it in your bath to boost your success level, courage, and creativity.

> ¼ cup bee balm flowers
>
> ¼ cup borage flowers
>
> ¼ cup clover flowers
>
> ¼ cup mullein flowers
>
> ¼ cup yarrow flowers
>
> ¼ cup shredded cabbage
>
> ⅓ cup columbine leaves
>
> ¼ cup sage
>
> 1 small chunk (about ½ inch by ½ inch) ginger, peeled and sliced
>
> 1 tsp. celery salt
>
> 1 chunk oak bark
>
> ½ cup pecans

Garden Magic Infusion

Use this infusion to water your house plants or walk the boundaries of your garden, sprinkling the infusion all around the garden boundaries. Visualize your plants growing tall and green and producing beautiful vegetables and flowers. Use the infusion to water fruit trees while envisioning the juicy fruits you want them to grow.

1 cup heather flowers

½ cup pansy flowers

½ cup alfalfa sprouts

½ cup pennyroyal leaves

½ cup sliced carrots

½ cup cyclamen root

1 chunk oak bark

2 large apples, sliced

1 banana, sliced

1 cucumber, sliced

½ cup figs

1 cup cut grapes

1 tsp. mustard seeds

¼ cup black olives

1 pomegranate, quartered

Home Blessing Infusion

Use this infusion to clean your house. Fill a gallon-size bottle with the infusion and walk around the outside of your house, pouring a path as you go.

4 oranges, sliced but not peeled

3 lemons, sliced but not peeled

4 chunks myrrh resin

4 chunks frankincense resin

The Least You Need to Know

- Infusions are the liquid resulting from boiling herbs to release their magical qualities. These potions can be prepared ahead of time, making them readily available when needed.

- When you use an infusion, your body absorbs the potion's magic, making it radiate from you.

- Infusions can be made with just about any kind of plant material, fresh or dried.

- Storing dried infusion blends is easy and convenient; however, remember to keep blends in a cool, dark place with as little air in it as possible.

- Infusions can be stored in the refrigerator or frozen to be ready for use at any time.

Oodles of Oils

In This Chapter

- Using oil-based potions
- Choosing and preparing ingredients
- Storing your oils
- Getting started with some recipes

Oils are my favorite potion ingredients to work with. One can use oils to create an endless variety of scents with surprising ease.

Oil Obsessions

If you are like me, you might find yourself becoming slightly obsessed with working with oils. They're so fun, in part, because they come in a variety of different forms, including essential oils, diluted oils, and infused oils.

The intended use of your potion dictates the type of oil potion you should make. I use essential oils, diluted oils, and infused oils all frequently. Oil potions make up an extremely large part of my practice.

Effortless Essential Oils

Essential oils are produced by removing the *volatile oil* from the plant material.

Magical Definitions _____

A **volatile oil** is an oil that contains characteristics of the flavor and scent of the plant from which it came.

Because large quantities of herb material are required and specialized equipment is needed to extract essential oils, it just isn't practical for you to attempt to do this on your own. It's perfectly reasonable and acceptable to buy your essential oils.

Unfortunately, some essential oils are extremely expensive. However, pure essential oils have a very long shelf life, and they will last for years if you are only using a very small amount at a time.

The best part of working with essential oils is the ease in using them. Most essential oils are sold either with an eyedropper fit into the bottle top, or with a nozzle that only allows a drop out at a time. And because you need only a tiny amount, if you don't like the way something smells, you don't waste much of the oil.

Enchanting Explanations

It takes approximately 30 rose buds to make 1 drop of essential oil. The price of rose oil runs about $35 per milliliter. Pure jasmine oil runs $45 for half an ounce, with sandalwood at about $35 for half an ounce.

I always recommend combining the essential oils before adding them to the carrier oil, so you have an idea of how the final product will smell. There's no sense in adding the essential oil mixture to the carrier oil and wasting the carrier oil if you don't like how it smells.

You can mix essential oils with one another and with carrier or infused oils to make your own perfect combinations. You can then use the mixtures in bath oil potions or perfume potions. Mixtures that don't contain carrier oils can be used in your diffuser or on the charcoal tablets.

No matter what you are mixing oils for, be sure to keep them in a bottle with a good, tight sealing lid to keep them fresh.

You can also find many of them already diluted with carrier oils.

Carefree Carrier Oils

Carrier oils include sweet almond oil, apricot kernel oil, grape seed oil, evening primrose oil, jojoba oil, sesame oil, sunflower oil, peanut oil, rose hip seed oil, coconut oil, hazelnut oil, safflower oil, peach kernel oil, and olive oil. These are nonvolatile oils. It is not generally recommended to use vegetable or corn oil, because of the smell, the thickness of the oil, and because they tend to go rancid quicker than the others.

Delightful Diluted Oils

Diluted oils are pure essential oils that have been added to a carrier oil. Diluted oils can either be made or bought. As stated earlier, pure essential oils that would be extremely expensive can be found in a diluted form. You can make your own diluted oils by adding a few drops of an essential oil to a carrier oil.

The label on a bottle of diluted oil should tell you the percentage of actual pure essential oil in the mix. For example, most rose oil mixes contain 5 percent essential rose oil, with the other 95 percent being the carrier oil. Just remember that if you add a diluted oil to a diffuser or lit charcoal tablet, you will be able to smell the carrier oil in addition to the essential oil.

Bathe and Glow

There aren't too many things I like better in this world than settling into a warm bath laced with magical oils. Oils in your bath serve two purposes: the scent the oils give off is released into the air, calling the magic to you; and, as the oil covers your skin, it also calls the magic into you. Basically, oils in your tub totally surround you with the magic you seek.

When adding oils to your bath, you can use any of the three types of oils—pure essential oils, diluted oils, or infused oils.

If you are using pure essential oils, a few drops will scent an entire bathtub. And keep in mind that essential oils are extremely potent, so always check for any allergens before adding them to your bath. Some oils carry a warning saying they might cause skin irritations; avoid adding these to your bath, or at the very least heavily dilute them with a carrier oil.

Toil and Trouble

Using oils in your bathtub can make the floor and sides of the tub dangerously slippery. When using oils in your bath, take extra caution when getting in and out of the tub, and use a cleaner that cuts the oil after each oil bath.

Because diluted oils also contain essential oils, you won't need much of these, either—about a tablespoon will do the trick.

Infused oils have the weakest scent of the bunch, so you can use more of this kind of oil in your water, but you don't want to use so much that you feel too greasy after your bath. Two tablespoons of infused oils should be plenty.

Simmer and Sizzle

Another of my favorite ways to use oils is to heat the oil and let the scent diffuse into the air. As the scent disperses around the room, it releases the magic into the air around you.

You can use an oil diffuser, or you can simply place a couple of drops onto a lit charcoal tablet in a censer. When using oils in either of these ways, use essential oils. Most carrier oils do not smell very good when they are heated or burned.

Some oil diffusers use electricity to warm the oil and others rely on the heat from a candle. Obviously, you need to take safety precautions with both.

Using an oil diffuser is easy. Place a few drops of the oil into the reservoir. If you're using an electric diffuser, the next step is simple: all you need to do is turn it on. If you're using a candle diffuser, place a lit tea light candle underneath the reservoir. Make sure the wick of the candle is trimmed so that the flame stays fairly low to avoid overheating the oil.

To diffuse your oils using a charcoal tablet, use an eyedropper to place a few drops of oil onto a lit charcoal tablet. Make sure to keep your face back, as the oil will produce a sudden burst of smoky steam. The scent is extremely potent—don't inhale it. As the steam and smoke rises, the magic is released into the air.

Performing Perfumes

You can make your own magical perfume oil blends by mixing essential oils and adding them to a carrier oil.

Perfume potions release magic into the air through their scent and draw the magic into the wearer. When you wear a perfume potion you create a sort of magical bubble that follows you around wherever you go.

Enchanting Explanations

History tells us the Egyptians were the first people to incorporate the use of perfumes into their daily lives as early as the eighth century B.C.E.

Because carrier oils can go rancid after a while, you might want to mix perfumes in small quantities, depending on how often you plan to use the potion. Make sure you use a bottle or vial with a tight sealing lid; this will help keep the perfume fresh longer.

Oil Infusions

An oil infusion is an oil that has been saturated with the magical properties of a specific plant by allowing that plant to soak in the oil.

Oil infusions can be taken internally (as long as the individual ingredients are safe for human consumption) or used externally.

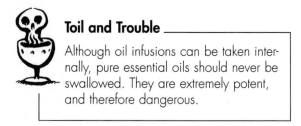

Toil and Trouble

Although oil infusions can be taken internally, pure essential oils should never be swallowed. They are extremely potent, and therefore dangerous.

Because this is an oil, you aren't going to want to drink large quantities of this type of potion. Children taking oil infusions should be given a teaspoon full, while adults can take a tablespoon.

Preparing infused oils is a relatively simple process, but it can require large quantities of ingredients, depending on how much of the infusions you want to prepare.

For your infusion preparations you will need fresh or dried herbs (fresh is better), canning jars, cheesecloth, a carrier oil, and a cool, dark place to store the canning jars for seven days. After the infusions are ready, you will need a wire mesh strainer, a bulb baster, and dark colored bottles with tight sealing lids.

Fashion Your Formulas

Infusions should be made with just one type of herb for each jar. You can create infusion combinations from individual infusions, but you need to start with a pure infusion.

Experiment with different carrier oils. You might prefer some for internal use and others for external use. Price might also be a factor when considering what type of carrier oil to use.

 Concoction Clues

> You can also mix carrier oils to create the perfect blend for yourself. Because oils can have different weights and consistencies, remember to gently shake them before each use.

Infuse Your Carriers

Begin with clean canning jars (the type with the lid and ring separate). If you have a dishwasher, run the jars through the dishwasher to make sure they are clean; otherwise, wash them in hot bleach water and rinse them well. Label the jars, indicating the kind of herb the oil will contain.

It really is best to use fresh herbs when making infusions, but if you don't have access to them and have to use dried herbs, make sure they have retained their color and scent for better results.

Prepare your infusions as follows:

1. Fill the jar three-quarters of the way full with the herb. Do not fill the jar all the way to the top and do not pack the herbs in tightly. Leave enough room in the jar so the oil can move freely around the herbs.

2. Pour oil over the herbs, filling the jar all the way to the top.

3. Place a piece of folded cheesecloth over the jar opening, using just the ring (not the lid) to hold it down tightly and secure it in place. Herbs sometimes give off gases, and the cheesecloth allows the infusion to breathe.

4. Store the jars in a cool, dark location for a week.

If you have the time, take a few minutes every day to replace the cheesecloth with the metal lid and gently shake the jar to mix up the herbs and oil. After shaking the jar, replace the metal lid with the folded cheesecloth. This helps to ensure all parts of the herbs are soaked in the oil.

Harvest Your Bouquet

After your infusions have set for a week, once again replace the cheesecloth with the metal lid and shake one more time.

Set a wire mesh strainer into a large bowl and empty the contents into the strainer. Use a spatula or even your pestle to squeeze any excess oil from the herbs into the bowl.

Simply discard the used herb material and get ready to bottle up your infusions.

Toil and Trouble

Unfortunately, herbs sometimes mold during the infusion process. If you find any signs of mold, you are going to have to throw the herbs and oil out and start all over again.

Bottle It Up

Using the baster, remove the oil from the bowl and squirt it into dark-colored bottles. These bottles should have tight sealing lids—either screw-on caps or tight-fitting corks—to help keep the oils fresh.

After your oil is bottled, label the bottles and store them in a cool, dark location. Infusions generally have a shelf life of about six months, but if you notice any changes in color or scent, discard the infusion and make another batch.

Blending Basics

Although an infusion can be used on its own—and you should make sure to try them in their pure state—you can also mix an infusion with other infusions to combine magical elements or to add to its magical potency, just like with other types of potions.

Start Simple

When you begin taking infusions internally, you'll want to use them in their pure unaltered state to get used to them. Some people have difficulty swallowing a teaspoon of oil—it's all a matter of taste.

Concoction Clues

> If you are using your oil infusions externally, you don't have to worry about taste, so forget about starting simple. Combine what you want and make your nose happy!

When you're ready to start blending your infusions, try mixing just two or three infusions together at first. And don't mix entire bottles, but just the amount you need at the time. You don't have to mix them in equal proportions, either. Try different combinations to discover what flavors you enjoy and provide the magical effects you seek.

Advanced Compounds

Advanced compounds involve combining four or more different infusions. As with simpler mixtures, make these in small doses so you can sample your concoctions without wasting a lot of infusions if it doesn't turn out as you had hoped.

After you find a taste you like, you can go ahead and mix up a larger amount of it, label it, and store it the way you store your other infusions.

If you don't plan to use your concoctions on a daily or weekly basis, I don't recommend mixing them up ahead of time. Instead, simply make them when you need them. And be sure to write down your exact ingredients so you can create the same potion time after time.

Let's Get Started

The following combinations will help you get started on your oil-making practices. For external potions, use essential oils; for internal potions, use infusions. Feel free to experiment and alter the recipes to suit your tastes and needs. Use your favorite carrier oils to make your infusions, and then combine the infusions as suggested in each of the following recipes.

Use as little or as much of each ingredient as you like to alter the taste or smell. Eliminate those ingredients you don't like.

When using these recipes in spell work, feel free to combine the different aspects. For example, before your spell work, take a bath in the appropriate oil, then sprinkle some of the corresponding oil on a charcoal tablet, and take a teaspoon or two of an appropriate infusion during your spell work.

Lose the Weight Oil

I wish I could tell you that this magical potion sheds the pounds without any additional effort on your part, but unfortunately, as with any kind of magic, we must live our mundane lives in accordance with our magical practices in order for them to work properly.

Clover	Pennyroyal
Ginger	Violet
Honeysuckle	Yarrow
Lemon balm	

Passion Perfume

Use these oils in different combinations to bring passion into your life.

Cardamom	Patchouli
Clove	Rose
Ginger	Sandalwood
Jasmine	Ylang-ylang
Lemongrass	

Negativity Be Gone Oil

Use combinations of these oils to disperse negativity in your life or a negative cloud that seems to be hanging around.

Basil	Bone set
Bergamot	Clove
Birch (young leaves)	Clover
Blessed thistle	Dragon's blood
	Elderberry

Frankincense   Witch grass

Mint   Yarrow

Mullein

Wish Swish

Combine and use oils from this list to help make
your wishes come true.

Allspice   Sandalwood

Bluebell   Star anise

Daffodil   Tonka bean

Dandelion   Violet

Ginseng

Energy Boosting Oil

Use any of these oils or infusions to give you an
energy boost.

Black pepper   Nutmeg

Camphor   Orange

Caraway   Patchouli

Carnation   Pennyroyal

Cinnamon   Peppermint

Garlic   Pine

Ginger   Saffron

Lemon   Vanilla

Lime

Good Luck Oil

Need a little extra luck? Try combining any of the oils or infusions from this list.

Allspice	Mistletoe
Bayberry	Nutmeg
Bluebell	Orange
Catnip	Strawberry
Ginseng	Vetiver
Irish moss	Violet

Broken Heart Mender Oil

When you need a little help getting over a broken heart, use any of these oils or infusions in a broken-heart-mender mixture.

Balm of Gilead	Cypress
Bayberry	Hyacinth
Calendula	Lily
Carnation	Rue
Columbine	Witch hazel
Costmary	

Friendship Fixer Oil

Have a fight with a friend? Combine these oils or infusions to help set things right.

Amber	Juniper
Apple blossom	Passionflower
Balm of Gilead	Rue
Basil	Slippery elm
Bayberry	Sweet pea

Self-Esteem Lifter Oil

When life is getting you down, combine these ingredients to help give your self-esteem a boost.

Amber	Honeysuckle
Bayberry	Hyacinth
Cinnamon	Lime
Ginseng	Orange
Grapefruit	Passionflower

If Adventure Had a Name Oil

Need a little adventure in your life? Or the courage to be a bit more adventurous? Mix these ingredients up to give yourself a boost.

Black pepper	Ginger
Carnation	Mullein
Cedar	Musk
Cinnamon	Onion
Clove	Peppermint
Columbine	Sweet pea
Fennel	Thyme

Open Communication Oil

Use a combination of these oils or infusions if you are having a communication problem with someone and you need to clear it up.

Caraway	Garlic
Cedar	Hyssop
Coffee	Lavender
Costmary	Lemon
Dill	Slippery elm

Visions Oil

Use these oils or infusions in any combination to experience magical visions.

Acacia	Lemon grass
Alder	Lilac
Angelica	Mace
Apple (wood)	Marigold
Bay leaves	Mugwort
Calendula	Nutmeg
Camphor	Oak (wood)
Carnation	Orange
Celery seed	Orris
Cherry	Patchouli
Cinnamon	Peppermint
Coltsfoot	Pine
Ginger	Poplar (wood)

Rose

Saffron

Star anise

Tangerine

Vanilla

Willow

Yarrow

Yerba santa

The Least You Need to Know

- Oils are used in three basic forms: essential, diluted, and infused.
- Essential and diluted oils are not safe for internal consumption.
- Perfumes, bath oils, and simmered oils release magic into the air, surrounding you in a magical bubble.
- Infusions can be taken internally, helping you draw the magic into you.

Tantalizing Tinctures

In This Chapter

- Using tincture potions
- Choosing and preparing ingredients
- Storing your tinctures
- Getting started with some recipes

Tinctures are yet another way of extracting the magical essence from herbs or flowers. A tincture is a mixture made from soaking plant material in alcohol or vinegar to absorb the plant's essence.

If you aren't big on oils, then you should definitively give tinctures a try. When the tincture is complete, you can either drink it (in a small dose), or dab it on your body or on an object, such as a magical tool, to anoint it.

Tincture Tactics

Tinctures are made by soaking herbs, flowers, or other plant material in a low-odor alcohol—such as vodka—or vinegar to extract the magical essence from the plant.

People differ in their approach to preparing tinctures—some prefer to measure ingredients precisely, while others believe one's own instincts serve them best. Either way, the final result will give you a true herbal tincture. It's a matter of personal taste as to how strong you want your tincture to be and what method you are more comfortable working with.

Enchanting Explanations

Although tinctures might have been used as far back as 900 B.C.E. in China, it was the sixteenth-century Swiss physician Paracelsus who made the use of alcohol as a solvent to make tinctures popular.

Tinctures are relatively inexpensive to make, especially if you grow your own herbs. They are far less expensive than many essential oils and, depending on the type of alcohol you use, might rival the cost of infusions. Alcohol tinctures also have a long shelf life, so they will stay fresh far longer than any other potion you make. (Pure, undiluted essential oils also have a very long shelf life.)

You can buy premade tinctures at most pharmacies or health food stores, but you can make your own tinctures at a fraction of the cost.

Because tinctures are so potent, you only need to use a small amount—anywhere from a couple of drops from an eye dropper to a teaspoon, depending on what feels comfortable to you. If you find the taste too strong, you can dilute your tincture by adding it to a cup of tea or a glass of water.

Tincture Preparations

Tinctures are easy to make, and the process is very similar to that of making oil infusions. You will need canning jars, a solvent (either alcohol or vinegar), herbs, and cheesecloth. You might also want to use a blender. You will also need a dark, cool location to store your tinctures while they set, along with dark colored bottles for storing them.

Open the Bar

Vodka is most often used when making tinctures, although you can use any type of alcohol that is at least 80 proof, such as rum or cognac, both of which help mask the taste of bitter herbs. It comes down to personal preference of taste and price.

 Concoction Clues

> Many different flavored vodkas are on the market these days. These can enhance the taste of your tinctures, or change the taste all together. You can experiment with different single-serving size bottles to find what you like best.

Vinegar Renditions

If you don't want to use alcohol in your tinctures, you can use vinegar instead. I highly recommend using plain white vinegar unless you really happen to prefer the flavor of a different vinegar. White vinegar is clear, making it easier to keep an eye on what is going on with your tincture while it is setting. With dark or cloudy vinegars, it's difficult to see whether the tincture develops any impurities as it sets.

Shake and Steep

When making your tinctures, you will need to decide whether or not to use exact measurements. With exact measurements, you will need 200 grams of dried chopped herbs for each liter of alcohol (or vinegar) or 300 grams of fresh chopped herbs per liter of alcohol (or vinegar).

If you aren't going to measure, use an amount you feel comfortable with. The more herbs you use, the more potent your tincture will be. Be careful not to pack the jar too tightly with herbs; you want the alcohol to be able to flow around the herbs.

If you have a blender available (preferably one that you use only for your magical workings), pour the herbs into the blender, followed by the alcohol. Make sure the herbs are totally covered in the alcohol, and then blend with the lid on for 60 seconds. Only use the blend setting—you don't want to puree the herbs or grind them into such small pieces that you can't strain them.

Pour the mixture into canning jars and top them off with more alcohol if needed. Seal the jars tightly and label with the contents and the date. Store the jars in a cool, dark location. You will need to have access to them on a daily basis, so pick a convenient spot.

At least once a day, shake the jars. The more frequently you can shake them, the better, with four times a day being optimal.

 Concoction Clues

> You can make your tincture preparations even more magical by working with the power of the moon. You might want to start your tinctures at the full moon (or new moon), allowing them to sit throughout the rest of the moon phases and then finish up on the next full moon (or new moon). You might even prefer to start your tinctures on the new moon and finish them on the full moon.

Depending on how strong you prefer your tincture, leave it set for anywhere from 2 weeks (this makes a weaker tincture) to a full 30 days.

Drain and Squeeze

After your mixtures have set for as long as you want them to, it's time to drain the alcohol off—this is your actual tincture.

Remove the lid from the canning jar and replace it with cheesecloth, using a rubber band to help hold the cheesecloth in place. Pour the liquid into a large bowl to reduce spills. When the jar is empty, hold it upside down and remove the cheesecloth, being careful to keep all of the herbs inside of the cloth. Hold the loose ends of the cheesecloth closed and squeeze the remaining alcohol from the herbs. Continue to squeeze until you can't remove any more liquid from the herbs. Discard the cheesecloth and herbs.

If you have one handy, you can use a crank style hand press, such as a wine press, to help remove as much of the alcohol or vinegar as possible.

Bottle It Up

Tinctures, like many of your other potions, should be stored in a dark colored bottle with a tight sealing cap or cork.

Using a baster, remove the tincture from the bowl and squirt it into the bottles.

Toil and Trouble

Because tinctures are made with alcohol, they can be flammable. Do not store them anywhere near a heat source such as a furnace or dryer.

Label your bottles, being sure to include the type of tincture and the date it was made. Store them in a cool, dark location. Tinctures will last a long time, up to two years, if stored correctly.

Blending Basics

Tinctures can be blended together as you see fit. You can make special combinations customized to your needs, or combine different herbs or tinctures to make your magical potion even more powerful.

Easy Does It

You can either add small amounts from different tinctures together, or you can mix up different combinations of the herbs to soak in the alcohol. If you mix different tinctures together, it is helpful if they are made with the same type of alcohol. If they are made with different types of alcohol, only mix up a small amount at a time.

When you first begin mixing herbs or tinctures, begin with combinations of only two or three, and begin increasing the ingredients as you discover what combinations are pleasing to your taste buds.

Advanced Concoctions

After you are familiar with different herbs and their flavor, feel free to experiment with more elaborate combinations to further specialize your practice.

You should still be careful on how many different types of alcohol you mix together, but feel free to experiment with different herbs. Keep track of your recipes as you go, and save those you like. Make sure you also keep track of combinations you don't like so you know not to make them again.

Let's Get Started

The one problem with tinctures is the amount of time you have to wait before getting your final results. There's no avoiding it, however, so it's best to get started right away. Use the amounts and ingredients you are comfortable with in any combination, or mix tinctures made from single ingredients.

The Green Eye of Envy

If you are having a problem with jealousy or envy, use this tincture on yourself. If you have a possession that you would like to protect from the envy of someone else, dab a little of this tincture on the item to protect it from the green eye of envy.

Angelica	Cedar
Bayberry	Clove
Bergamot	Columbine
Blessed thistle	Costmary
Burdock	Cowslip
Camphor	Cypress

Dill

Fennel

Hawthorn

Nettle

Slippery elm

Shy No More

Although some people might be shy and enjoy their privacy, others want to break out of their shells. This mixture is designed to help get you out into the world.

Bee balm

Borage

Chervil

Chickory

Columbine

Mullein

St. John's wort

Thyme

Yarrow

Get Your Creative Juices Flowing

Sometimes you just need a jump-start to get your creativity in gear. Use these herbs in any combination to get your brain storming.

Angelica

Borage

Chicory

Coltsfoot

Elecampane

Galangal

Mullein

Pansy

Periwinkle

Rose

Sage

Savory

Thyme

Yarrow

Yerba santa

Travel Happy

Prepare this tincture before going on a trip, and take it with you, stored in a spill-proof bottle. Carrying the potion with you helps to keep you safe from harm. If you are driving, sprinkle some of the tincture on the tires before you leave.

Amaranth	Eucalyptus
Basil	Feverfew
Blackberry	Hyssop
Burdock	Lavender
Celandine	Linden
Clove	Marjoram
Comfrey	Mint
Dill	Primrose

Brightest Blessings

This tincture is designed to be used before performing a ritual. It can also be used to consecrate magical tools.

Anise	Echinacea
Apple (either the bark, wood, or fruit)	Fennel
	Lavender
	Lemon
Chamomile	Parsley
Chervil	Rose
Clover	Thyme
Coconut	

Spirituality

Use this tincture before or during rituals or spell work to increase your spirituality through connection with the Gods and/or Goddesses.

Angelica

Apple (either the bark, wood, or fruit)

Bay

Camphor

Carnation

Cedar

Celery seeds

Cinnamon

Coltsfoot

Daffodil

Dandelion

Gardenia

Ginger

Mullein

Yarrow

Tranquil Moments

Use this tincture to release your mind from stress and worries to help you relax. You can add a couple of drops to bath water or use a corresponding oil mixture for best results:

Basil

Bee balm

Bergamot

Calendula

Chamomile

Coltsfoot

Freesia

Gardenia

Hyacinth

Jasmine

Lavender

Lemon balm

Marjoram

Meadowsweet

Passionflower

Rose

Violets

Ylang-ylang

Fear Factor

Fear is something we all deal with at some time or another. This tincture is designed to help you cope with your fears while you work at getting over them.

Angelica	Mullein
Borage	Pennyroyal
Calendula	Savory
Chervil	St. John's wort
Chicory	Thyme
Clover	Yarrow
Columbine	

Lift Self-Doubt

This tincture is for when you just aren't sure if you can trust your own instincts. It's for occasional situations when you might doubt yourself.

Borage	Onion
Calendula	Pennyroyal
Celery	Rose
Coltsfoot	St. John's wort
Jasmine	Thyme
Lettuce	Yarrow
Mullein	

Obstacle Remover

Use this tincture when you encounter one of life's many hurdles and you need a little help getting over it.

Amaranth	Dill
Angelica	Heather
Blackberry	Irish moss
Celandine	Linden
Chicory	Loosestrife
Clove	Marjoram
Columbine	

Negativity Ban

Use this tincture to keep the negativity of other people from crowding into your space. Dab a little on your pulse points.

Angelica	Elderberry
Aspen	Frankincense
Bee balm	Hawthorn
Bergamot	Holly (leaves)
Birch (wood)	Horehound
Cedar	Juniper
Clove	Nettle
Clover	Pine
Dragon's blood	

Love in the Air

Use this tincture to help bring love into your life. Dab a little bit on your pulse points.

Bee balm	Lavender
Chamomile	Pansy
Clover	Periwinkle
Coltsfoot	Primrose
Ginger	Rose
Heather	Ylang-ylang
Jasmine	

The Least You Need to Know

- A tincture is made by allowing herbs or other plant material to steep in alcohol for a minimum of two weeks.

- You may substitute the alcohol with vinegar for a nonalcoholic tincture.

- Tinctures are safe to consume as long as all of the ingredients used to make it are safe to consume.

- Tinctures are extremely potent and can last up to two years.

- Tinctures are taken in small doses—from a few drops up to a teaspoon.

Chapter **8**

Luscious Lotions

In This Chapter

- Using lotion potions
- Choosing and preparing ingredients
- Storing your lotions
- Getting started with some recipes

Making your own lotion potions enables you to customize the lotion to smell the way you want and, of course, have the magical properties you desire.

The Sensuality of Lotions

Lotions, through their effect on your senses of touch and smell, can help you create a particular mood. The scent of a lotion can put you into different states of mind through aromatherapy. Lotions also help you enter a state of consciousness simply through the feel of the lotion on your skin, especially if you work intimately with a magical partner. Rubbing lotion onto each other's skin creates a whole new sensation.

Lotion Applications

Applying lotion can be an utterly sensual experience. If you use a magical lotion, you are drawing the potion's magic into your body and releasing it into the air around you. And, of course, lotions also moisturize your skin.

Enchanting Explanations

There are many ways to make your own lotions, ranging from incredibly simple to somewhat complicated. Personal preference for ingredients and the amount of time and work you want to put into your potions will dictate what method you use.

You can increase the power of a potion by applying it after taking a bath suited for the same need. For example, if your goal is to draw money to you, soak in bath oils designed to attract money and follow it up by applying a lotion designed to attract money. By using many different potions at the same time or in succession, you increase the magic several times over, making it extremely powerful.

Special Effects

Have some fun and personalize your lotions using special ingredients. For example, give yourself a shimmery look by adding some glitter to your lotion. Pick a color that matches the lotion's magical intent. Combine glitter of different sizes and colors to create more complex lotions and add to their magical properties.

By adding corresponding colors (see Appendix B), you incorporate more magical elements into your potion. You might also want to pick up some little bags of metal confetti from a party supply store. When added to your lotion, the tiny confetti will stick to you (for a while) when you apply the lotion. Look for confetti that goes along with your intent.

Concoction Clues

Check at your local craft store to find a large assortment of glitter. Glitter is available in hundreds of different colors, with sizes ranging from very fine powder to larger chunks.

Instead of—or in addition to—adding colored elements such as glitter and confetti to your lotion, you might want to consider coloring the lotion itself. Many local craft stores sell coloring that can be used when making soaps or lotions. This coloring is safe and will not stain or discolor your skin. Pick a color that corresponds with your intent.

Lotion Production

By far the quickest and easiest way to make magical lotions is to begin with a bottle of premade lotion and modify it to suit your needs. A large bottle of unscented cocoa butter lotion is a great place to start.

Divide the lotion into several small bowls to be bottled up as separate lotions later. Personalize each bowl of lotion for a different need by adding essential oils to infuse your lotion with the magical properties you want it to contain. If you can't find an essential oil that corresponds with your need, you can use an oil infusion or tincture. You can then add corresponding coloring, glitter, and/or confetti if you wish. Pour each bowl into its own bottle and label it. How's that for simple!

Gather Together

If you'd prefer to make your lotions from scratch, you have a number of choices. The recipe you use will dictate the ingredients you use, but you'll need a few basic ingredients and supplies for most recipes.

For starters, you need some sort of heat source to melt ingredients together. You can use either a microwave with microwaveable dishes or a stove with a double boiler. If you don't have a double boiler, a pot filled with water and an empty metal coffee can make a handy substitute.

You will also need wooden spoons, a blender or wire whisk, a funnel, a candy thermometer, and bottles for storing your lotions.

Your basic ingredients will include distilled water, a carrier oil, an *emulsifier*, (some stores carry their own brand of emulsifier, or you can use borax) and essential oils (or infused oils or tinctures). For carrier oils, consider using grape seed oil, coconut oil, olive oil, or almond oil. You might also want to buy chunks of cocoa butter, shea butter, and beeswax. You can also add vitamin E oil or food grade aloe vera gel to your lotions.

Magical Definitions

An **emulsifier** is a substance that keeps water and oil from separating when mixed together.

Other ingredients your recipes might call for include vegetable glycerin, borax, candelilla wax, carnauba wax, liquid lecithin, palm wax, palm oil, or palm kernel oil. These items can be found at your local grocery or health food store.

Melt the Solids

If you decide to use cocoa butter, shea butter, or beeswax, (or any other waxes), you must first melt them on the stove or in the microwave. You then add your choice of oil and gently heat the mixture to allow the ingredients to blend together.

Toil and Trouble

Never allow any of these ingredients to get too hot; keep them from splattering and possibly burning you. It is possible for some of these ingredients to catch fire, so never leave them unattended while being heated. When using the stove, always keep the flame on low.

When melting ingredients, start with beeswax because it will take the longest to melt. If using the microwave, only run the microwave for a couple of minutes at a time and stir the wax before restarting the microwave. As the beeswax begins melting more (or if you are using only a small amount) cut the time down to 30-second intervals and stir between each run. Never allow waxes or butters to boil.

Cool Down

You will need to let your mixture cool slightly (5 minutes or so) before adding it to the ingredients in your blender. After it has cooled slightly, pour it slowly into the blender. If you have to use a wire whisk, it will take you much longer to complete your lotion, and you will probably want to allow your mixture to cool a bit more for safety reasons.

Bring on the Blender

While your butters or waxes are melting, prepare your other ingredients. First, add the water; if you are using aloe vera gel, vitamin E oil, borax, or vegetable glycerin, add those now, and blend at the highest speed for about 30 seconds.

Pour in the wax or butters and blend on a low speed for about a minute to allow some of the heat to escape. Turn the blender up to the highest speed and blend for 5 minutes. If the mixture starts to get too thick, stop.

Add the essential oils, infused oils, or tinctures you want to use. If you want to add any colorings, glitter, or confetti, add these now and continue blending on high for another minute, scraping the sides as needed.

The mixture will begin to thicken, and you will be able to tell by looking at it when the mixture is ready.

If you are mixing by hand, add the water (aloe vera gel, vitamin E oil, borax, or vegetable glycerin if needed) to a bowl and start whipping as you add the other ingredients. It would be helpful if you had someone pour ingredients while you do the whipping.

Pour and Store

To finish up, all you need to do is pour your lotions into labeled bottles. In order to do this with the least amount of mess, use a funnel that fits into your bottles. You can also try using a baster to squirt lotion into bottles.

If your lotions don't have a preservative, such as citric acid, they will last about two months. Do not store lotions in the refrigerator; they should be kept at room temperature so none of the ingredients harden and leave you with a chunky mess.

Toil and Trouble

You'll know your lotions are going bad when they begin to smell rancid. Eventually they will either get really runny or harden, depending on the ingredients.

Let's Get Started

Essential oils give lotions their magical properties, and you can personalize any of the lotion recipes included in this section just by changing the essential oils that the recipe calls for. You can also add essential oils to premade lotion to create magical lotion potions.

Enchanting Explanations

After you've practiced with a few recipes in this chapter, you might be ready to expand your lotion-making practice. Don't be afraid to try new recipes. You might even want to invest in a book that specializes in homemade lotions.

Legal Maneuvers

Use this lotion whenever you have a court appearance or are dealing with any type of legal matters, such as making a will or signing mortgage papers.

Start with an 8-ounce bottle of premade cocoa butter lotion with no scent added.

1. Pour all of the lotion into a bowl.
2. Add two drops of each of the following oils, infusions, or tinctures:

   Buckthorn oil

   Cascara sagrada oil

   Celandine oil

   Marigold oil

   Brown coloring (optional)

3. Stir the mixture and pour it into the original bottle.

Astral Projection

This lotion should be used before undertaking an *astral projection* session to help get you into the proper mindset and to ensure a safe and productive trip.

Magical Definitions

Astral projection is the practice of entering into a trancelike state in order to project your spirit to other locations.

Assemble the following ingredients:

> 1 cup distilled water
>
> 1 cup almond oil
>
> 2 TB. liquid lecithin
>
> 1 drop angelica oil
>
> 5 drops basil oil
>
> 1 drop damiana oil
>
> 1 drop dittany of crete oil
>
> 2 drops mugwort oil
>
> Indigo or blue coloring (optional)

Prepare the lotion:

Combine water, almond oil, and lecithin in a pot on the stove over low heat until it is well blended and warm. Remove from heat and allow to cool before blending in the oil drops and coloring. Store in a glass or plastic bottle.

Memory Enhancer

Use this lotion whenever you need to give your memory a boost. It can be particularly helpful when studying for a test. Apply the lotion when you're studying the material and again when taking the test.

Assemble the following ingredients:

> ½ cup almond oil
>
> ½ cup grape seed oil
>
> 1 cup distilled water

2 TB. liquid lecithin

1 drop caraway oil

1 drop eyebright oil

5 drops lily of the valley oil

3 drops rosemary oil

1 drop spearmint oil

Blue or yellow coloring (optional)

Prepare the lotion:

Over low heat, combine almond oil, grape seed oil, distilled water, and liquid lecithin in a sauce pan. Heat thoroughly. (You should see a slight steam coming from the mixture.) Allow to cool to room temperature and add essential oil drops and coloring. Mix well and pour into bottles.

Spiritual Grounding

This lotion should be used before doing any spiritual work such as meditations, spells, divinations, or rituals. Ideally, this lotion should be applied after taking a ritual or cleansing bath.

Assemble the following ingredients:

2 oz. cocoa butter

6 oz. grape seed oil

1½ cups distilled water

5 drops frankincense oil

5 drops myrrh oil

Black, purple, or silver coloring (optional)

Prepare the lotion:

1. Melt the cocoa butter in microwave or double boiler, stirring frequently.

2. Pour melted cocoa butter into a blender and add grape seed oil and water. Blend ingredients together.

3. Add frankincense oil and myrrh oil and blend until mixed.

Headache Eradicator

Use this lotion to help relieve headaches. You can apply the lotion all over your body, but pay special attention to massaging the lotion into your temples and forehead.

Assemble the following ingredients:

1 oz. cocoa butter

1 oz. shea butter

6 oz. almond oil

1½ cups distilled water

2 drops amber oil

6 drops bergamot oil

1 drop chamomile oil

1 drop lemon oil

Green or white coloring (optional)

Prepare the lotion:

1. Melt cocoa butter and shea butter in microwave or double boiler, stirring frequently.
2. Pour melted mixture into a blender and add almond oil and distilled water. Blend ingredients together.
3. Add remaining ingredients and blend until mixed.

Serenity Haven

Try this relaxing lotion for relieving stress and easing your mind. It's particularly effective after a relaxing bath.

Assemble the following ingredients:

1 oz. beeswax

4 oz. shea butter

8 oz. almond oil

1½ cups distilled water

3 drops apple blossom oil

3 drops freesia oil

3 drops hyacinth oil

5 drops lavender oil

3 drops lily of the valley oil

3 drops narcissus oil

Blue, pink, or white coloring (optional)

Prepare the lotion:

1. Melt beeswax and shea butter in microwave or double boiler, stirring frequently.
2. Pour melted mixture into a blender and add almond oil and distilled water. Blend ingredients together.
3. Add remaining ingredients and blend until mixed.

Bad Luck Terminator

Suffering from a string of bad luck? Use the bad luck terminator to help set things right again.

Assemble the following ingredients:

1 oz. beeswax

3 oz. cocoa butter

3 oz. shea butter

⅓ cup olive oil

⅓ cup almond oil

⅓ cup grape seed oil

2 cups water

10 drops vitamin E oil

1 drop allspice oil

1 drop bayberry oil

1 drop bluebell oil

1 drop catnip oil

2 drops ginseng oil

2 drops Irish moss oil

2 drops nutmeg oil

8 drops rose oil

Green coloring (optional)

Prepare the lotion:

1. Melt beeswax, cocoa butter, and shea butter in microwave or double boiler, stirring frequently.

2. Stir in olive, almond, and grape seed oils.

3. Pour water into blender. Add oil mixture and vitamin E oil. Blend ingredients together.

4. Add remaining ingredients and blend until mixed.

Pleasant Dreams

Chase away nightmares and other unpleasant dreams with the pleasant dreams lotion. This lotion will also help you remember your dreams when you awake.

Assemble the following ingredients:

2 TB. beeswax

½ cup olive oil

½ cup almond oil

¼ tsp. borax

½ cup distilled water

2 drops bergamot oil

2 drops calendula oil

10 drops jasmine oil

2 drops mugwort oil

Blue coloring (optional)

Prepare the lotion:

1. Melt beeswax in microwave or double boiler, stirring frequently.

2. Stir in olive oil and almond oil.

3. Pour mixture into blender. Add borax and distilled water. Blend ingredients together.

4. Add remaining ingredients and blend until mixed.

Glimmer Glamour

Use this lotion when you want to feel glamorous. Be sure to add some sparkly glitter to this one!

Assemble the following ingredients:

1 oz. cocoa butter

1 oz. shea butter

1 oz. beeswax

1 oz. coconut oil

2 oz. jojoba oil

2 oz. vegetable glycerin

10 oz. distilled water

2 drops ginseng oil

6 drops lilac oil

2 drops orange blossom oil

2 drops rose oil

Red coloring (optional)

Glitter (optional)

Prepare the lotion:

1. Melt cocoa butter, shea butter, and beeswax in microwave or double boiler, stirring frequently.

2. Stir in coconut oil, jojoba oil, and vegetable glycerin.

3. Pour mixture into blender. Add distilled water. Blend ingredients together.

4. Add remaining ingredients and blend until mixed.

Psychic Enhancer

Use this lotion before performing psychic workings, such as divinations or readings.

Assemble the following ingredients:

3 TB. beeswax

½ cup olive oil

½ cup grape seed oil

½ cup almond oil

3 cups distilled water

1 tsp. borax

1 drop acacia oil

5 drops cinnamon oil

1 drop honeysuckle oil

1 drop iris oil

1 drop lemongrass oil

2 drops mugwort oil

1 drop peppermint oil

1 drop rose oil

1 drop tangerine oil

2 drops wormwood oil

Purple coloring (optional)

Prepare the lotion:

1. Melt beeswax in microwave or double boiler, stirring frequently.

2. Stir in olive, grape seed, and almond oils. Set aside.

3. Pour distilled water and borax in blender and blend together. Add oil mixture and blend again.

4. Add remaining ingredients and blend until mixed.

Divine Inspiration

Need a creative boost? This lotion will help you find the inspiration you crave.

Assemble the following ingredients:

2 tsp. shea butter

2 tsp. candelilla wax

¼ cup evening primrose oil

¼ sunflower oil

¼ cup avocado oil

¼ cup olive oil

½ tsp. borax

2 tsp. vegetable glycerin

4 cups water

1 drop angelica oil

1 drop cowslip oil

3 drops daffodil oil

1 drop dandelion oil

3 drops gardenia oil

1 drop lotus oil

1 drop mullein oil

3 drops myrrh oil

1 drop primrose oil

1 drop violet oil

Yellow coloring (optional)

Prepare the lotion:

1. Melt shea butter and candelilla wax in microwave or double boiler, stirring frequently.

2. Stir in evening primrose oil, sunflower oil, avocado oil, and olive oil.

3. Pour mixture into blender. Add borax, vegetable glycerin, and water. Blend ingredients together.

4. Add remaining ingredients and blend until mixed.

Celestial Protection

The ultimate in protection lotions, use this potion whenever you feel you need protection, such as when doing magical workings, or if you feel threatened in any way.

Assemble the following ingredients:

2 TB. beeswax

¼ cup shea butter

⅓ cup grape seed oil

⅓ cup coconut oil

⅓ cup almond oil

⅓ cup aloe vera gel

⅔ cup distilled water

10 drops vitamin E oil

1 drop blessed thistle oil

5 drops dragon's blood oil

5 drops frankincense oil

2 drops hyssop oil

4 drops myrrh oil

White coloring (optional)

Prepare the lotion:

1. Melt beeswax and shea butter in microwave or double boiler, stirring frequently.

2. Stir in grape seed oil, coconut oil, and almond oil. Set aside.

3. Pour aloe vera gel, distilled water, and vitamin E oil into blender and blend together. Add oil mixture and blend again.

4. Add the remaining ingredients and blend until mixed.

The Least You Need to Know

- Lotions surround you with a magical bubble as they draw the magic into you.

- When making magical lotions, you can start with premade lotions and add magical ingredients or you can start from scratch.

- Lotions can be used when working intimately with a magical partner to increase the power and energy, and therefore the magic.

- Homemade lotions without preservatives have a shelf life of about two months.

Beguiling Beverages and Brews

In This Chapter

- Using beverage potions
- Choosing and preparing ingredients
- Storing your beverages
- Getting started with some recipes

Although a cup of tea can be relaxing, sometimes you need something more potent, whether to cure what ails you, overcome an obstacle, or simply create a feeling of goodwill. Not only will the magical properties of the beverages and brews in this chapter help you achieve many of your goals, they taste great, too!

Raise a Glass!

You can drink these potable potions to fill a specific magical need or simply to celebrate magical times with friends. It all depends on the drink being prepared and your intention as you prepare it.

A Taste Sensation

The recipes in this chapter are sure to please your taste buds as well as your senses! The first 10 recipes are intended to be mixed in small batches—a glass or pitcher at a time—for your personal use. These beverages have a very short shelf life—in most cases just a matter of days, even when stored in the refrigerator.

 **Concoction Clues** _____

> For maximum magical potency, use the freshest ingredients you can find. For example, freshly squeezed fruit juices have a higher concentration of magical properties than canned, processed fruit juices.

The remaining 10 recipes are drinks for magical celebrations such as rituals or festivals. The recipes will make enough of the beverage to serve a larger number of people. Most of these recipes contain alcoholic ingredients or are intended to be mixed with alcohol. They should be used the same day they are made.

Individual Instructions

Although each recipe has a distinct set of instructions, they all share one direction in common: make them with a heart full of love for yourself and for those you will be serving.

Enchanting Explanations

Home brewing is a fun hobby that will also save you a ton of money on alcoholic beverages. A six gallon cask of mead will save you a minimum of $160 when compared to buying bottles of mead at the store. With home brewing, you can also create different flavor combinations that are next to impossible to find in stores. If you are really interested in home brewing, there are many books available on the subject. The only down side to brewing your own wines is having to wait for them to ferment!

Let the Merriment Begin

I recommend making these drinks strictly by the instructions until you are familiar with them, especially the brews. After you've made a recipe a few times, though, feel free to experiment.

Concoction Clues

Make the most out of your magical experience by inviting your guests to help you make the mixed drinks. Each person can add a different ingredient while saying a heartfelt statement of thanks or requesting a specific blessing.

Dieter's Delight

Start your day off on the right foot with this tasty—
and healthy—concoction. It's packed with lots of
good stuff and will give you plenty of energy to
make it through the day. Use this drink in place of
your regular breakfast to help you lose weight.

Assemble the following ingredients:

$\frac{1}{2}$ banana sliced

$\frac{1}{4}$ cup orange pulp

$\frac{1}{4}$ cup sliced strawberries

$\frac{1}{4}$ cup raspberries

1 cup apple juice

Prepare the ingredients as follows:

Put all ingredients in blender and puree until
smooth.

Ambrosia Aphrodisiac

This drink is designed for two people to share during a night of romance.

Assemble the following ingredients:

$\frac{1}{2}$ cup papaya juice

$\frac{1}{2}$ cup pear nectar

$\frac{1}{2}$ cup pineapple juice

$\frac{1}{4}$ cup cherry juice

$\frac{1}{2}$ cup sliced bananas

½ cup chopped mango

½ cup chopped kiwi

1 cup crushed ice

Prepare the ingredients as follows:

Put all ingredients in blender and puree until smooth. Pour into two wine glasses and top with whipped cream and a maraschino cherry.

For a little extra kick, add two shots of vodka to this drink before pouring it into glasses.

Stress Buster

When you just need to wind down and chill out, mix this drink up, sit back, kick off your shoes, and relax as you let the stress melt away.

Assemble the following ingredients:

3 cups brewed chamomile tea, slightly cooled

1 tsp. freshly grated ginger

4 fresh mint leaves

1 splash of vanilla

Prepare the ingredients as follows:

1. Using a food processor or mortar and pestle, finely grind ginger and mint leaves.
2. Pour ground mixture into blender, and add chamomile tea and a splash of vanilla.
3. Puree mixture until well blended.

Purifying Juice

This potion is meant to purify your body both physically and spiritually. Drink it 24 hours before performing a ritual, spell, or other magical working.

Assemble the following ingredients:

> 2 cups cranberry juice
>
> ½ cup prune juice
>
> Juice from one freshly squeezed lemon

Prepare the ingredients as follows:

Mix ingredients together and sip throughout the day. This one is tart, so it might make you pucker up a bit!

Truth Be Known Elixir

Although this drink sounds like something you might want to sneak to someone to find out if they are lying to you or not, that's not really its intent. Instead, you should slip yourself some of this potion to find the truth inside you. After drinking this potion, find a quiet spot to sit and meditate.

Assemble the following ingredients:

> 2 cups brewed sage tea
>
> 1 apple
>
> 1 TB. cherry juice

Prepare the ingredients as follows:

1. While focusing on the question or problem at hand, cut the apple into quarters and place three of the quarters inside a large glass.

2. Pour cherry juice over the apples, then add sage tea.

3. Sip this drink as you meditate over the answer you are seeking.

Spiritual Ecstasy

Use this drink before performing rituals, spell work, divinations, or spiritual meditations. It is designed to open your heart and mind spiritually.

Assemble the following ingredients:

½ cup cherry juice

½ cup grape juice

½ cup orange juice

½ cup apple juice

½ cup papaya juice or nectar

Prepare the ingredients as follows:

You can either pour all the juices into a blender or mix them together in a small pitcher by hand.

Creative Shove

If you are like me, you'll want to mix up a pitcher of this potion. Whenever I need some creativity, I always make it in large doses!

Assemble the following ingredients:

> 4 cups papaya juice or nectar
>
> 1 cup crushed pineapple with juice
>
> ½ cup sliced bananas
>
> ¼ cup raspberries
>
> ¼ cup blackberries

Prepare the ingredients as follows:

Combine all ingredients in a blender and puree until smooth.

Love Fruit Juice

Prepare this juice when you are looking for love. This juice will help draw love to you.

Assemble the following ingredients:

> ½ cup apple juice
>
> ½ cup chopped apricots
>
> ½ cup orange juice
>
> ½ cup papaya juice or nectar
>
> ½ cup pear juice
>
> ½ cup raspberries
>
> ½ cup strawberries

Prepare the ingredients as follows:

Blend all ingredients together. On a hot summer day, add a cup of crushed ice.

Healthy Hit

This healthy concoction is made using nuts. Grind the nuts finely in a food processor before adding them to the blender.

Assemble the following ingredients:

> 2 cups apple juice
>
> ⅛ tsp. ground allspice
>
> 1 tsp. finely ground walnuts

Prepare the ingredients as follows:

Add ingredients to blender and mix thoroughly. Drink immediately, as this beverage doesn't store well.

Money Bags

Use this drink when you are looking for a bit of cash to come your way. The almonds should be ground finely before adding them to the rest of the drink.

Assemble the following ingredients:

> 1 tsp. finely ground almonds
>
> 1 cup blackberries
>
> 1 tsp. ground cashews
>
> ½ cup crushed pineapple
>
> 2 cups apple juice

Prepare the ingredients as follows:

Add ingredients to blender and mix thoroughly. Drink immediately, as this beverage doesn't store well.

Midsummer Faery Wine

This is the perfect wine to accompany your Midsummer ritual feasts. When the faeries come out to play, we all get a little magical feeling.

Use this easy recipe to flavor wine with lavender flowers. For each bottle of white wine you will need 1 cup of lavender flowers and some cheese-cloth.

Pour the wine into a large pitcher. Pour the lavender flowers onto a piece of cheesecloth and bunch it into a pouch. Tie some string around the cheesecloth to keep the lavender inside. Throw the cheesecloth into the pitcher and let it set overnight in the refrigerator. Serve chilled.

Eggnog

Eggnog is a traditional drink for the winter holidays. Instead of buying it in the store, try making it yourself this year.

Assemble the following ingredients:

6 eggs

12 TB. sugar

2 cups milk

1 cup brandy

2½ tsp. vanilla

¼ tsp. salt

2 cups heavy whipping cream

3 tsp. nutmeg

Prepare the ingredients as follows:

1. Separate eggs, storing the whites in the refrigerator until needed later.
2. Beat the yolks while adding 6 tablespoons of the sugar, until the mixture is thick and creamy.
3. Add milk, brandy, vanilla, and salt, and mix well.
4. Store the egg yolk mixture in the refrigerator to chill.
5. Beat egg whites until peaks form, and then add the sugar until you have stiff peaks.
6. Combine the egg whites with egg yolk mixture and heavy whipping cream.

Serve immediately sprinkled with nutmeg. Because this recipe contains raw eggs, make sure it doesn't sit out for too long.

Samhain Remembrance

This is the perfect drink to accompany your feast following your Samhain ritual. Have different guests add each ingredient as they share a memory of a loved one who has gone on before them.

You will need a large pot for preparing this drink. If it is at all possible for you to make it in a cauldron over an open fire, do it!

Assemble the following ingredients:

Small handful of cloves

Apples (without peeling them, slice the apples so that the pentagram shape formed by the seeds shows)

Oranges (without peeling them, slice the orange and remove any seeds)

1 gallon apple cider

1 TB. grated ginger

4 cinnamon sticks

Prepare the ingredients as follows:

1. Insert a couple of cloves in each apple and orange half.

2. Pour the apple cider into the pot on low heat or in a cauldron over a small fire.

3. Add the ginger, cinnamon sticks, and fruit slices. Ask your guests to participate in adding the orange and apple slices.

4. Heat the cider without bringing it to a boil. It should be warm and steamy.

If possible, drink the cider while standing around a bonfire.

Spring Wine

This is an easy recipe for flavoring a bottle of white wine. The resulting fun and fruity wine is perfect for your Beltane celebrations.

Assemble the following ingredients:

> 1 bottle of strawberry-banana juice
>
> 1 bottle of white wine
>
> 2 cans of pear nectar
>
> 1 pint fresh sliced strawberries

Prepare the ingredients as follows:

1. The night before, pour the strawberry-banana juice into ice cube trays and freeze it. Also, chill the pear nectar and white wine.

2. Before your celebration, pour the white wine into a punch bowl.

3. Add the pear nectar and the strawberry-banana ice cubes.

4. Pour in the sliced strawberries and stir.

Chamomile Wine

This is another simple but delightful recipe for perking up a bottle of white wine. You will need a large airtight container for steeping the mixture for a week.

Assemble the following ingredients:

> 1 bottle of white wine
>
> 1 cup dried chamomile flowers, or 6 chamomile tea bags
>
> 2 TB. lemon zest
>
> 3 TB. honey

Prepare the ingredients as follows:

Mix all ingredients together in a large airtight container. Seal the container and store in a cool, dark location for a week. Strain the chamomile and zest from the wine with cheesecloth and serve.

Honey Mead

Honey mead has got to be my favorite drink in the world. After preparing this recipe, I think you'll understand why! For this recipe, you will need a cask.

Assemble the following ingredients:

> 4 gallons water
>
> 8 cups honey
>
> 1 cup lemon juice
>
> 1 tsp. nutmeg
>
> 4 packages brewer's yeast

Prepare the ingredients as follows:

Heat the water, honey, lemon juice and nutmeg in a large pot on the stove, stirring occasionally to mix all ingredients together and dissolve the honey. Stir in the brewer's yeast, then pour the mead into a cask.

Let the mead ferment in a cool, dark location for 6 months. You will also need to "burp" the mead daily to allow any built up gases to escape. How do you burp the mead? The cask you buy will come with instructions on just how to do this. Some casks have a stopper you pull out to allow the gases to escape, others you may have to remove the entire lid. If you don't burp your mead, you run the risk of having your cask explode.

Blackberry Wine

Blackberries can be expensive, but if you grow your own, this is an excellent recipe to try. You will need a cask for this recipe.

Assemble the following ingredients:

   5 pounds blackberries

   2 gallons water

   10 cups sugar

Prepare the ingredients as follows:

1. Put the berries in a large bowl and cover it with cheesecloth. The berries need to sit at room temperature and rot for four weeks. Make sure you stir them up every couple of days. You might notice they begin to mold, but this is okay.

2. After four weeks have passed, put the berries into a blender and puree until they are liquefied.

3. Bring the water to a boil and, while stirring, add the sugar, making sure it dissolves thoroughly.

4. Add the blackberries to the boiling water and blend thoroughly.

5. Pour the wine into a cask and let it ferment for 10 to 12 months. You will need to burp the cask every day to allow the built up gases to escape.

Dandelion Wine

This wine doesn't need to ferment nearly as long as some of the other homemade wines in this chapter. This is a quick recipe that doesn't take long to make and enjoy.

Assemble the following ingredients:

½ gallon dandelion flowers

2 gallons water

8 pounds sugar

7 lemons, peeled, seeded, and cut in half

1 package brewer's yeast

1 slice of toast

Prepare the ingredients as follows:

1. Boil the dandelion flowers for a half an hour and strain them, reserving the water. Discard the flowers.

2. Add sugar to the strained hot water and stir until thoroughly dissolved.

3. Put the lemon halves into the cask and pour sugar water over them.

4. When the water has cooled to 92 degrees (use a thermometer to check), pour the yeast onto the toast and set it on top of the water mixture.

5. Let the mixture set for 2 to 3 days. Remove the toast and skim off any yeast on top of the wine. Pour wine into a punch bowl and serve.

Hot Buttered Rum

Hot buttered rum is a wonderful drink for cold-weather parties, as it will warm you all the way to your toes. It's easy to make and is perfect for a crowd.

Assemble the following ingredients:

4 cups water

2 cups unsalted butter (do not use margarine)

2½ cups brown sugar

1¼ cup powdered sugar

3 tsp. nutmeg

3 tsp. cinnamon

½ gallon vanilla ice cream

1 750 ml bottle of rum

Prepare the ingredients as follows:

1. Heat the water to boiling and add the butter.

2. On low heat, allow the butter to melt completely, then add the brown sugar, stirring until it is dissolved.

3. Add the powdered sugar, nutmeg, and cinnamon, stirring until dissolved.

4. Turn off the stove and remove the pan from the heat.

5. Quickly scoop the entire ½ gallon of ice cream into the pot and pour the rum over the top. Stir quickly to mix.

6. Immediately pour into mugs and top with whipped cream.

Wassail

This is the perfect drink for your Yule celebrations. Again, this is meant to serve a large crowd.

Assemble the following ingredients:

1 gallon ale

2 TB. nutmeg

2 TB. ginger

2 TB. cinnamon

1 TB. grated lemon peel

12 eggs

2 cups powdered sugar

1 gallon brandy

Prepare the ingredients as follows:

1. Add nutmeg, ginger, cinnamon, and lemon peel to ale and warm the mixture without bringing it to a boil.

2. While the ale is heating, beat eggs with powdered sugar.

3. Add eggs to ale and stir slowly.

4. Add brandy and serve.

The Least You Need to Know

- You can make all different kinds of beverages with a magical intent. You need only know the magical properties of the ingredients you are using.

- You can add to your magical experiences by having a group of people help prepare the magical drink. Each person contributes a part of themselves and a part of their own magic to the final product.

- Home brewing saves you money and gives you the opportunity to create beverages you wouldn't be able to find elsewhere.

- Remember to burp wines that require it to prevent casks from exploding. Always follow your recipe and the instructions for your cask.

Glossary

amulet   An object worn or carried to ward off negative energies. An amulet may be blessed with a potion during a ritual to give it extra power.

anoint   To bless an item with a consecrated liquid.

asperger   A bunch of fresh herbs used to sprinkle a magical liquid during a ritual or spell. The herbs are saturated with the liquid and then shook to dispel the liquid around a given area.

astral projection   The practice of entering into a trancelike state in order to project your spirit to other locations.

boline   (bow-LEEN) A knife with a curved blade used to harvest and cut herbs.

book of shadows   A book in which you keep track of all of your magical workings including spells, rituals, and recipes. You will want to keep a copy of your potion recipes in your book of shadows.

carrier oil   A carrier oil is also known as a base oil or vegetable oil that does not contain a strong fragrance. They are called carrier oils because they "carry" essential oils.

censer A nonflammable container used for burning incense or a charcoal tablet.

charging The process of infusing an object, item, or potion with personal power.

cleansing Removing negative energies from an object, person, or place.

components The supplies used in magical workings that need to be replenished, such as herbs, oils, and incense.

consecration Blessing, cleansing, and positively charging an item for magical use.

diluted oils Oils that are made by adding a few drops of an essential oil to a carrier oil.

emulsifier A substance that makes water and oil mix together without separating.

esbats Rituals held at the new and full moons.

essential oil The pure volatile oils removed from a plant.

familiar A spirit who takes the form of an animal and helps the witch or magician in their magical practices.

incense Powdered herbs and resins combined for their magical properties. Incense can be in the form of a powder, cone, or stick and is burned to release the magic into the air.

infusion The liquid extract that results from boiling herbs to release their magical qualities.

intent The main ingredient in your potions. You must know why you are making the potion and what it is you want it to do.

Neo-Pagan   The term used to describe modern-day people who practice a religion similar to the Pagans of the past; literally means "new Pagan."

oil infusion   An oil that has been infused with the magical properties of a specific plant by allowing that plant to soak in the oil.

Pagan   The Latin word meaning "country dweller," it now refers to one who practices a polytheistic religion, which many of the country dwellers did.

potion   A combination or mixture of components which contain either medicinal or magical properties.

pulse points   The places on your body where you can feel your pulse through your skin such as on your neck or wrist below the palm of your hand.

purification   To cleanse something or someone spiritually, removing any and all negative energies.

resin   The hard (or semi-hard) deposit left by plant sap.

ritual   A ceremony of celebration. Rituals can be performed for sabbats, esbats, or other special occasions. A common element to rituals is that of giving thanks.

rootstock   Another name for a rhizome.

sabbats   The eight Pagan holy days. These include Yule, Imbolg, Ostara, Beltane, Midsummer, Lughnasadh, Mabon, and Samhain.

scrying   A divination process in which the person (scryer), stares into a reflective surface seeking images and visions. Some potions can be poured into a dark colored bowl and used to scry in.

sigil A magical symbol similar to a logo; you can create your own sigil and add it to your potion labels.

spell Similar to the Christian version of prayer. A spell combines many different elements and correspondences that are directly related to the request being made.

steep To soak plant material in a liquid to move the plant's essence from the plant into the liquid.

talisman A magically charged object that is designed to bring about certain energies. A talisman can be charged with a potion during a ritual.

tincture A mixture made from soaking plant material in alcohol or vinegar to absorb the plant's essence.

volatile oil An oil that contains characteristics of the flavor and scent of the plant from which it came.

witchdoctor A person who uses magic to cure illnesses.

Color Correspondences

Often in this book, I suggest that you use coloring that corresponds with your magical intent to help increase the power of your potion. Here is a list of colors with their magical correspondences:

black absorbs negative energies, banishes, binds, eases confusion, defines boundaries, divination, protection, and minimizes loss.

blue (dark) astral projection, change, hope, honor, healing, fidelity, protection, truth, tranquility, psychic abilities, sleep, peace, dreams, unity, wisdom, knowledge, and represents the virgin Goddesses.

blue (light) calmness, tranquility, good health, patience, and understanding.

brown earth, stability, neutrality, balancing, concentration, grounding, strength, decision making, pets, family issues, justice, integrity, sensuality, endurance, and grace.

gold represents the God, strength, success, courage, action, vitality, solar Goddesses, summer, wealth, the sun, power, daylight, employment, and masculinity.

grey neutrality, absorbs negative energy, visions, anger, envy, and greed.

green abundance, money, growth, prosperity, healing, fertility, employment, luck, jealousy, appearance, neutralizing, calming, financial matters, career, and security.

indigo changes, flexibility, visions, psychic abilities, and insight.

orange pride, ambition, courage, enthusiasm, energy, adaptability, the sun, attraction, will power, imagination, success, friendship, communication, and opportunities.

pink love, romance, affection, tenderness, harmony, compassion, spiritual healing, spring, peace, honor, morality, virtue, contentment and success.

purple insight, inner strength, inspiration, spirituality, growth, self-esteem, psychic abilities, power, ambition, success in business and physical fitness.

red lust, passion, sexual love, fire, will power, courage, energy, strength, anger, life cycles, desires and blood.

silver spiritual truth, the Goddess, intuition, inner self, femininity, moon power, night, balance, stability, and receptivity.

turquoise honor, idealism, discipline, self-knowledge, and creativity.

violet healing, deep sleep, intuition, self-improvement, spiritual awareness, and success.

white purification, innocence, childhood, truth, divination, protection, peace, cleansing, tranquility and healing.

yellow vitality, happiness, persuasion, study, mind power, for exams and tests, psychic abilities, charm, creativity, intelligence, communications, and attraction.

Potion-Making Resources

If you don't live near a metaphysical or health food store, it may be difficult to come by some of the ingredients and equipment you need to make your potions. The following is a list of companies you can either find on the Internet or call for a catalog.

AB Container
21 Manning Road
Enfield, CT 06082
1-800-229-2914
www.abcontainer.com

AB Container sells bottles and jars in an assortment of sizes for potion storage.

Avalon Apothecary
www.avalon.cc

Avalon Apothecary specializes in bulk herbs, tinctures, oils, and teas.

Bramble Berry, Inc.
2138 Humboldt Street
Bellingham, WA 98225
360-734-8278
www.brambleberry.com

Bramble Berry is a supplier of essential oils, fragrance oils, and lotion-making ingredients.

Cat's Lair
www.lairofthecat.com

Cat's Lair is a source for different premixed oil blends.

eBottles.com
1764 Litchfield Turnpike
Woodbridge, CT 06525
1-888-215-0023
www.ebottles.com

eBottles is another source for bottles or jars to store your potions in.

The Enchanted Attic
23 E. Columbia Ave.
Battle Creek, MI 49015
269-963-3125
www.the-enchanted-attic.com

The Enchanted Attic sells an assortment of items including herbs, essential oils, and premixed fragrance oils.

Herbs and Arts
2015 E. Colfax Avenue
Denver, CO 80206-1303
303-388-2544

Herbs and Arts sells a large assortment of bulk herbs.

Isis Books and Gifts
5701 E. Colfax Avenue
Denver, CO 80220
1-800-808-0867
www.isisbooks.com

Isis books carries herbs, herbal guides, essential oils, carrier oils, and an assortment of books on aromatherapy.

Kamala
1-877-424-1963
www.kamala.com

Kamala specializes in premixed fragrance oils but also carries some essential oils, tea blends, and bulk herbs.

Majestic Mountain Sage
918 West 700 North Suite 104
Logan, UT 84321
435-755-0863
www.thesage.com

Majestic Mountain Sage carries a ton of products related to lotion making, from oils and additives to glitter.

Mission Peak Soap Products
PO Box 2086
Fremont, CA 94536
510-795-1326
www.missionpeaksoap.com

Mission Peak Soap Products carries lotion-making supplies and carrier oils.

Mother Nature's Emporium
3023 N.E. Adams
Peoria, IL 61603
www.mothernaturesemporium.com

Mother Nature's Emporium is a virtual online mall. Here you will find several different stores carrying herbs, essential oils, carrier oils, and several other potion-making ingredients.

Mountain Rose Herbs
PO Box 50220
Eugene, OR 97405
1-800-879-3337
www.mountainroseherbs.com

Mountain Rose Herbs carries a large variety of herbs and carrier oils.

Nemat International, Inc.
27365 Industrial Blvd, Suite K
Hayward, CA 94545
1-800-936-3628
www.bestbottles.com

Nemat International is another source for bottles and jars.

Nyvens Destiny
954-557-0462
www.nyvensdestiny.com

Nyvens Destiny carries a large variety of essential and blended fragrance oils.

Otherworld Apothecary
www.otherworldapothecary.com

Otherworld Apothecary sells an assortment of herbs, resins, teas, and oil blends.

Pine Meadows
860 N. 1430 W.
Orem, UT 84057
801-221-0483
www.pinemeadows.net

Pine Meadows sells fragrance oils, essential oils, and lotion-making supplies.

Savouré
www.savoure.com

Savoure carries tea blends, tea bags, and tea brewing equipment.

Scent Sanctuary
519-874-4048
www.scentsanctuary.ca

Scent Sanctury carries herbs, essential oils, carrier oils, bottles and jars, fragrance oils, lotion-making supplies, and tons of other supplies and equipment you can use in your potion-making practices.

Shop Wicca
PO Box 2180
White City, OR 97503
www.shopwicca.com

Shop Wicca carries oil blends and herbs.

Specialty Bottle LLC
5215 Fifth Avenue S.
Seattle, WA 98108
206-340-0459
www.specialtybottle.com

Specialty Bottle LLC offers a huge assortment of bottles.

Spray Bottles
407-891-8624
www.spraybottles.com

Spray Bottles carries an assortment of spray bottles ideal for body sprays or cleaning potions.

Index